FINDING CULTURAL ACUITY

PALMETTO
PUBLISHING
Charleston, SC
www.PalmettoPublishing.com

Copyright © 2024 by Darryl Washington, D.Ed.

All rights reserved

No portion of this book may be reproduced, stored in a retrieval system, or transmitted in any form by any means–electronic, mechanical, photocopy, recording, or other–except for brief quotations in printed reviews, without prior permission of the author.

Hardcover ISBN: 9798822969124
Paperback ISBN: 9798822969131

FINDING CULTURAL ACUITY

KNOWING YOURSELF AND
UNDERSTANDING YOUR
INFLUENCE

DARRYL WASHINGTON, D.ED.

DEDICATION

I dedicate this book to my extraordinary grandparents, Grandma and Grandad, who first introduced me to the profound beauty of unconditional love. Despite living in a world that may not have afforded them complete dignity and respect, these humble and kind souls embodied grace and propriety in every sense. Their quiet strength and unwavering decency left an indelible mark on my heart. I remember them with deep affection, and I hope this work serves as a small step toward erasing prejudice, marginalization, and exclusion in honor of their legacy.

ACKNOWLEDGMENTS

I extend my deepest gratitude to Dr. David Livermore, who honored me with the opportunity to become a cultural intelligence fellow. Without this induction, this book would not exist. His genuine, affirming presence encouraged me to embark on this transformative writing journey. His belief in me ignited the spark that brought these words to life.

I am also grateful to my friend Eugenia Roberts, whose unwavering support pushed me to confront the weight of my racial identity and the suppressive force it can hold over life. Her insight and encouragement were invaluable in this process.

Thank you both for your lasting impact on this work and me.

TABLE OF CONTENTS

CHAPTER ONE

"I SEE BECAUSE I SAW." 1
    Unconnected 1
    The Wondrous Years 5
    No Technicolor? 8
    "There's Gray Area?" 14
    Include Me, Not My Race 17
ACUTE TRANSFORMATION 21
Reflection Questions—Chapter One 23

CHAPTER TWO

BEING AND BELONGING 24
    "To Whom Am I Belonging?" 24
    To the Victor, No Spoils 25
    Truly Belonging? 27
    Belonging: Who Decides? 33
    "Othered, Then Belonging" 35
Reflection Questions—Chapter Two 42

CHAPTER THREE

PSYCHOLOGY IS TO CHICKEN AS CULTURE IS TO EGG . 43
    False Assertions Entrap People 43
    You Bias Me, I Bias You 48

Precursors to Bias: Understanding the Subconscious Forces
Shaping Our Perceptions 50

Bias by Reason. 54

Reflection Questions—Chapter Three 59

CHAPTER FOUR

"WHY CAN'T THEY SEE AS I SEE?". 60

I Am Black?. 60

The Pain of Code-Switching .62

Changelings 65

"The Defiant Ones" 70

Classic Black versus Neo-Black. 72

African Identity?. 76

Reflection Questions—Chapter Four 83

CHAPTER FIVE

FROZEN IN MIND: THE PSYCHOLOGY OF CULTURAL
SUPPRESSION 84

Impact of Cultural Suppression 84

What is Cultural Suppression Anyway?. 90

Indigenous American Reflections on Cultural Suppression. . .91

Development of Cultural Acuity. 101

Reflection Questions—Chapter Five. 103

CHAPTER SIX

FINDING CULTURAL ACUITY 104

    Cultural Intelligence: The Engine That Can 104

    Culturally, Intelligently Driven 112

    Feelings Drive CQ 114

    CQ Drive in Motion 118

Reflection Questions—Chapter Six 123

CHAPTER SEVEN

WHAT IS IT THAT YOU DO NOT UNDERSTAND? 124

    Culturally Knowledgeable 124

    Knowing versus Feeling Culture 127

    Devoid of CQ 129

    Ethnocentrism Rejects CQ Knowledge 134

    Valueless 136

Reflection Questions—Chapter Seven 149

CHAPTER EIGHT

CQ STRATEGY: SEE NO EVIL, HEAR NO EVIL, SPEAK NO EVIL 150

    Intelligence Strategy 150

    Thinking about Thinking 153

    The Cupper Sisters' Epiphany 155

    Humility: The Ultimate Culturally Intelligent Strategy ... 158

Reflection Questions—Chapter Eight 163

CHAPTER NINE

CULTURALLY APPROPRIATE ACTIONS 164
    Adapting, We Will Go 164
    Cultural Fluency 168
    Remember Me 171
    "The Salad Bowl" 176
Reflection Questions—Chapter Nine 180

CHAPTER TEN

BIGGER THAN MYSELF 181
    Growth Opportunities 181
    Sincerely Held Beliefs 187
    Globalism or Culturally Distinct? 191
    Hear Differently: Sociopolitical Effects on Individual
    Psyches 193
Reflection Questions—Chapter Ten 197

ABOUT THE AUTHOR 198
NOTES 199

CHAPTER ONE

"I SEE BECAUSE I SAW."

Unconnected

One of my earliest memories is steeped in a peculiar sense of detachment, as though I existed both within the moment and as an observer outside of it. I was just two years old, yet I can still vividly picture myself toddling alongside my mother through the sprawling expanse of a shopping mall. The corridors seemed to stretch endlessly; towering ceilings accentuated their enormity, making everything feel impossibly vast. My small world, bound by the comforting presence of my mother, suddenly seemed unfamiliar and overwhelming.

Her face is etched in my mind, softened by exhaustion, her eyes carrying a quiet, unspoken plea. She eased me from her hip with a weary tenderness and lowered me onto the cool, hard tiles. "You can do it," she whispered gently, her tone laced with encouragement and resolve. For a fleeting moment, I stood there, unsteady and unsure, as though the ground beneath me had shifted. My legs wobbled beneath

FINDING CULTURAL ACUITY

the weight of an unfamiliar independence, and the air around me felt uncertain.

We moved forward together, though my steps were clumsy and hesitant. My small hand brushed against her blue-patterned smock as I struggled to keep up, my protests growing louder with each step. "Up, Mom, up!" I pleaded, my arms reaching for the familiar comfort of her embrace. Nevertheless, she did not relent. Her pace remained steady, her calm voice urging me onward. There was a firmness in her encouragement that I couldn't comprehend then—a quiet insistence to learn to take those steps independently. For the first time, my world felt vast and unkind, no longer confined to the protective sphere of her arms.

Only years later did I understand the weight of her weariness that day. She was about six months pregnant, a fact that had been entirely lost in my young mind. Her rounded belly was another part of her, no more significant than her hands or voice. I couldn't grasp that she was carrying more than her exhaustion; she was carrying my baby brother, and at that moment, she was teaching me my first quiet lesson about letting go.

At the time, I could not articulate the strange swirl of emotions within me—confusion, frustration, and a profound sense of detachment. Overwhelmed, I burst into tears, whimpering echoing in the cavernous mall. Sensitive even then, I was acutely aware of her reaction. Sensing her patience waning, I quickly stifled my cries, swallowing my feelings to avoid a reprimand. It was an early lesson in restraint that would replay in different forms throughout my life.

This memory marked a subtle shift in our relationship. The closeness I had known began to feel more tenuous, and in the days that followed, that distance crystallized into one of the most poignant experiences of my young life. In his little blue Simca, my father took my brothers and me for a ride. Mom had been absent from home for several days—a mystery to me then. When she reappeared, she carried a bundle swaddled tightly in a blanket. To my astonishment, it was a baby—my baby brother.

Excited to see her, I lunged forward from the back seat to greet her, eager to understand this new addition to our lives. However, her response was abrupt. "Sit down, get back, and stop breathing on the baby," she said, her voice firm. Her words stung, and I felt my place in her world shift at that moment. It was as if I had been relegated to the back seat—not just of the car, but of life itself.

Looking back, these early experiences etched deep impressions on my understanding of relationships and my place in the world. They were the building blocks of my evolving self-perception, shaping how I viewed my connection to others. My mother, my first and most significant bond, was the cornerstone of my early existence. Every need, fear, and comfort found its anchor in her presence. She was my protector, my guide, my sanctuary.

One day, a different kind of memory unfolded in the familiar embrace of her parents' home. My great-uncle Alphonzo had come to visit, and the house buzzed with the hum of conversation. As Granddad and Uncle Alphonzo sat sipping cocktails, the mood was jovial, their laughter filling the room. However, when my mother entered, the atmosphere shifted. Perhaps emboldened by their drinks, they began teasing her, their laughter becoming playful jests. Their antics escalated, and they chased her around the dining table, their behavior crossing an invisible line in my young mind.

A surge of fear and indignation rose within me. I wanted to defend her and stop the teasing, but I was too small and powerless. My only recourse was silent pleading—a fervent wish for their taunts to cease. Sensing my distress, my mother intervened, her firm words ending their jesting. In that moment, I realized the depth of my protective instinct toward her, even if my actions were limited to the strength of my unspoken will.

These early memories remain vivid, their threads woven tightly into the fabric of who I am. They taught me vulnerability, resilience, and the delicate balance of dependence and independence. Most of all, they reminded me of a mother's love's profound and enduring impact, even when expressed in the quiet lessons of letting go.

My parents divorced when I was around eight years old. Before that, we were a typical family unit with Mom, Dad, myself, and my three brothers, with me being the third born. Like many middle children, I often felt overlooked, caught between the attention given to the eldest and the youngest. It sometimes felt like I was just an extra in the family dynamic. Now, as a parent myself, my perspective has shifted. I have come to understand that my love for each of my children, including my middle child, is equal and unwavering. True love knows no favoritism; it is impartial and unconditional.

Despite my siblings and parents' presence, I often yearned for a deeper connection, typically seeking solace and understanding from my mother. I trailed her every move, seizing any chance to be in her company, as it was through these moments that I perceived a richer layer of life experience unfolding. While initial impressions are crafted within the confines of the nuclear and extended family, I recognize that subsequent layers of experience emerge from our interactions with the broader society.

As we grow older and accumulate experiences, our grasp of human interactions deepens. However, in our earlier years, navigating relationships beyond our immediate circle can be a confusing journey marked by incomplete perspectives.

Before starting kindergarten at the age of four and a half, my world was confined primarily to the safety of my home, where interactions revolved around my parents, siblings, and occasionally, extended family, mainly grandparents. While this environment provided comfort, it limited my exposure to diverse relationships and perspectives outside my family unit.

Familial perceptions and interactions largely shaped my sense of self during this period. Despite these connections, I often felt isolated and a lack of genuine care or affection from those around me. Thus, while my familial sphere provided security, it left me yearning for deeper connections and a broader understanding of relationships beyond my immediate circle.

The Wondrous Years

In my early years, I observed the daily routines of my family members. While my brothers and dad headed out for school and work, my mom and I typically stayed home. I would watch as she diligently went about her tasks—vacuuming, cooking, dusting, and tending to household chores. The television often served as background noise during these moments, though my mom rarely paid much attention. Occasionally, I would catch glimpses of daytime programs, including soap operas, game shows, and what seemed to me to be ominous news broadcasts.

As I grew older, I began to grasp the unsettling nature of the news, which often featured stories of wars, assassinations, and events involving people who resembled my family members. These reports left me

FINDING CULTURAL ACUITY

with a lingering sense of unease, as the content rarely conveyed anything positive or reassuring. As the time came for me to embark on the same daily routine my brothers had already experienced, I entered kindergarten. Beyond the excitement of new toys, my feelings toward this new chapter were mixed. While I appreciated the opportunity to interact with classmates and forge connections, my primary fascination was exploring the unfamiliar environment.

Among the various activities, I found solace in the child-sized replica kitchen, perhaps because it resonated with the domestic tasks I associated with home and my mother. Engaging in pretend cooking and cleaning allowed me to feel a sense of familiarity and comfort amid the novelty of kindergarten. However, one aspect stood out: my kindergarten teacher, Ms. Pollard. Unlike my classmates, she was an older Caucasian woman whose demeanor left much to be desired. To my young mind, she appeared stern, if not outright mean. I could not help but wonder if her demeanor stemmed from frustration, possibly due to the school's transition from a predominantly white neighborhood to a predominantly black community. Perhaps she felt out of place or constrained by the changes.

Reflecting on my experiences with Ms. Pollard, I recall a striking pattern within the school's administration. While she and the principal shared a Caucasian background, the teaching staff boasted a more diverse demographic. Initially overshadowed by my perception of Ms. Pollard's demeanor, this observation revealed deeper implications.

Ms. Pollard's behavior left a lasting impression on me in kindergarten. Despite my efforts to behave, her frequent communications with my parents painted a picture of me as a problem child. Her critiques, often unwarranted, focused on trivial aspects of my speech and behavior.

One particular incident stands out vividly in my memory: Ms. Pollard's insistence that I undergo special classes for speech therapy. This recommendation led my parents to seek the expertise of a speech pathologist whose assessment contradicted Ms. Pollard's assertions. To my relief, the speech pathologist deemed me perfectly fine, prompting my mother to agree that no further sessions were necessary.

However, rather than accepting this professional opinion, Ms. Pollard's attitude seemed to sour further. She resorted to a campaign of nitpicking, sending home notes with increasingly absurd criticisms. One such note addressed the pronunciation of my name, suggesting a "correction" from "Darrell" to "Darryl," presumably to fit her preferences.

Even more troubling was her insinuation regarding my behavior in the toy kitchen. Rather than appreciating my imaginative play, she implied that it hinted at effeminacy, leading to a misguided discussion between my mother and aunt about preventing such tendencies. Consequently, I was instructed to avoid the toy kitchen altogether and focus on playing with what she deemed "boy stuff."

Upon reflection, these incidents exposed Ms. Pollard's biases and shed light on the societal pressures and stereotypes that shaped her perceptions. Her actions not only shook my confidence but also perpetuated harmful gender norms. On other occasions, her evident dislike left a lasting mark on my psyche, making me hyperaware of how others might perceive me. I struggled to comprehend what I had done to provoke her apparent disdain.

One particularly memorable event occurred in Ms. Pollard's kindergarten class during our midday nap. As we settled down, each of us finding a spot on the floor with our mats, I found myself restless, craving activity rather than sleep. Despite the dimmed lights and enforced silence, I could not shake off my alertness. Feeling the grit of the dirty floor beneath me, the warmth of the room, and the suffocating pressure of silence, I began to idly trace patterns on my mat, creating a rhythmic noise with my fingernails. Though not particularly melodic, it served as a distraction from the boredom.

Ms. Pollard's reaction was swift and furious. "Get up!" she barked before ushering me to a supply closet and locking me in. Frightened, I pounded on the door, demanding to be released. Eventually, after my cries stirred the entire class, she relented and let me out. To compound my humiliation, she sent a scathing letter home to my parents, resulting in the harshest punishment I had experienced up to that point: a severe spanking from my father.

Ms. Pollard marked my foundational encounter that underscored the disparities between " Black " and "White." Nevertheless, grappling with the underlying reasons remained elusive. The quest for understanding, for comprehending why her demeanor toward me was tainted with disdain, gradually unfurled as my social horizons expanded. Through myriad interactions, the patterns emerged. In the dynamics between Black and White individuals, a disconcerting trend surfaced: while White counterparts exuded confidence and authority, responses from Black peers often felt subdued, relegated to a position I perceived as inferior.

No Technicolor?

My mother catalyzed my journey into recognizing racial disparities. With her Caucasian appearance, featuring traits typical of Northern European ancestry, and my 19 percent Scottish heritage suggesting a similar lineage, she epitomized this background. In stark contrast, my father bore the visage of African descent, his complexion darker, hinting at a different lineage. Despite my mother's undeniable beauty by any measure, she often endured the sting of onlookers' scolding remarks, questioning her choice of partner with phrases like, "How could you marry such an ugly man?" Later, upon deeper reflection, I grasped the underlying implication rooted in ethnicity.

I was not my mother's favored child but her eager assistant, especially during our grocery shopping outings. Saturday mornings often found us amid long queues at the checkout counter, where my mother meticulously placed the divider on the conveyor belt to demarcate our groceries from those of the previous customer. As she engaged in amiable chatter with the cashier, I lingered behind, ensuring all our items were neatly arranged for the tally.

Nevertheless, despite my presence and the lack of a divider where I stood, the cashier routinely handed my mother the bill without acknowledging the items I had placed. Each time, my mother would politely interject, "Oh, those are mine too," eliciting a terse "Oh" in response. The once-congenial exchange would abruptly cease, the transaction proceeding in a somber silence. These experiences taught me that my brown skin triggered this shift in social dynamics. I grappled with overwhelming guilt, feeling responsible for my mother's embarrassment. It pained me to witness her love for me seemingly diminish. It begged the haunting question: What could I do with my black face to evade such treatment?

Spending time with my paternal grandparents was always a cherished experience. They showered my brothers and me unconditionally, making every moment spent with them feel special. Despite lacking material possessions coveted by others, they epitomized the essence of simplicity and contentment.

FINDING CULTURAL ACUITY

I vividly recall their humble abode from my childhood days. Nestled on a parcel of rented land, their home was a testament to their resilience and perseverance. Their landlord, an elderly woman, hired them to do everything from grass mowing to ironing and entrusted them with domestic chores in exchange for their modest dwelling. Situated amid vast fields, their residence, by American standards, could be described as a three-room shack, its weathered facade bearing witness to years of neglect and decay.

However, amid the clutter of accumulated possessions due to their tendency to hoard, their home exuded warmth and familiarity. Long before thrift stores became fashionable, friends and acquaintances generously contributed items to my grandparents, ensuring they lacked nothing beyond life's necessities.

Visiting my paternal grandparents offered a sobering glimpse into the enduring echoes of the Antebellum South, where racial and social divisions lingered like unyielding ghosts. Imbued in a culture deeply rooted in agrarian traditions, ideals of chivalry, and a wistful longing for a bygone era, I confronted the stark reminders of history—especially the haunting legacy of chattel slavery.

Their city bore the weight of its past, a place where the auction blocks once stood, where groups of enslaved African Americans were routinely sold to the highest bidder. The recent removal of an eight-hundred-pound sandstone block, once a public display of this dark history, could not erase the city's deep-rooted ties to its past. It remained a stronghold of institutional racism, a testament to centuries-long struggles against systemic oppression.

Every aspect of life seemed to carry the weight of history. The interactions between my grandparents and individuals of different races and social classes revealed a stark contrast. It was a lesson in the unspoken rules of societal hierarchy, where phrases like "Stay in your place" resonated with chilling clarity.

It was a poignant reminder of the enduring shadow cast by an outlawed class system. The disparities in treatment and expectations based on race were unmistakable, serving as a powerful testament to the lasting impact of historical injustices. In those moments, I grappled with the complexities of identity and belonging, confronted by the harsh realities of a past that continued to shape present-day dynamics.

When the sun rose, I rose with it, a trait that seemed to resonate with Grandad. I cherished the opportunity to accompany him on his errands, for he was a man of perpetual motion, often stirring with the dawn. We embarked on a journey where each stop held a purpose, usually involving his many odd jobs, or he would stop at each workplace to pick up his modest earnings.

One particular stop stands out vividly in my memory: the "wash rack," a local car wash. Here, Grandad assumed the responsibility of maintaining the parking area, ensuring its tidiness and orderliness. He meticulously emptied trash cans into the dumpster, and then came the highlight for me: scouring the vacuum cleaner trash containers. This task was special because a treasure trove of coins lay hidden within the dust and debris. People seemed prone to spilling loose change in their car seats, and Grandad made it a habit to collect these stray coins. He proudly displayed cups filled with these salvaged treasures by his bedside, a testament to his resourcefulness and the value he found in life's small fortunes.

After finishing up at the beloved wash rack, Grandad often made stops at other homes where he had worked, typically doing lawn maintenance. These visits had a familiar pattern: he would be greeted at the back door, his typical Caucasian employer offering him cash or a check, but not before a friendly exchange of pleasantries and sometimes a shared laugh over a prior conversation. As a mere visitor, I observed the rhythm of these interactions, noticing a sense of familiarity that seemed to carry from one employer to the next. Grandad was a congenial man, effortlessly charming and witty, never meeting a stranger.

However, a shift in tone and demeanor was palpable when Grandad engaged with another African American. There was a noticeable ease, a casualness absent, in the conversations with his Caucasian employers. Gone were the "yes sirs" and "yes ma'ams," replaced by a more relaxed atmosphere where laughter was uproarious and genuine, not the controlled "ha ha" of propriety. Even without fully understanding it at the time, I sensed an unspoken dynamic of superiority and inferiority in these exchanges between Grandad and his Caucasian employers.

There was a particular employer that Grandad often took my brothers and me to visit whenever we found ourselves in the heart of their southern Confederate town. Despite Grandad being obliged to use the back entrance for entry and payment and engaging in the customary pleasantries, there was a noticeable absence of the typical superior-inferior dialogue. This employer, whom we knew as "Audrey," bore a name typical of her generation but defied traditional female appearances. She exclusively wore trousers and a button-up shirt, with both hands habitually tucked into her pockets. Audrey's gait was assertive and purposeful, characterized by broad strides and squared shoulders, traits not often associated with a traditional Southern lady. Her movement conveyed a sense of directness and efficiency, with a slight swing of the arms adding to the impression of straightforwardness.

In contrast to Grandad's interactions with other employers, Audrey addressed him differently, speaking to him as a peer rather than employing the usual superior tones. This was fitting, considering their shared generation and longstanding residency in the same town for most of their lives.

Audrey opened my eyes to the intricate dynamics within Black and White relationships. Despite coming of age during a time when African Americans faced systemic oppression, she transcended these constraints, embracing a broader view of humanity. To her, everyone, regardless of race, deserved dignity and respect. Through her influence, I began questioning the injustices I perceived in society.

As a child, opportunities for meaningful dialogue with adults were rare, but Audrey's presence emboldened me. I vividly recall one day when my grandad and I visited her house to collect his pay, entering through the customary back door. Audrey, always warm and fond of me, initiated her usual conversation, asking about school and other topics she thought might interest a child.

In a moment of boldness, I turned to my grandad and innocently questioned why we always entered through the back door wherever we went. My question seemed to catch him off guard, leaving him speechless and visibly flustered. Unaware of the discomfort I had caused him, I unwittingly stepped into a minefield.

However, Audrey, quick to diffuse the tension, intervened gracefully. With a gentle smile, she redirected my curiosity, asking if I wanted to see the front of her house because of its beauty. Eager to explore, I affirmed, and Audrey, with her characteristic warmth, took my hand and led me on a tour of her home.

In that moment, Audrey demonstrated that not all White people viewed me as inferior. Her kindness and understanding left a lasting impression, teaching me valuable lessons about empathy, respect, and the potential for positive change, even amid entrenched social norms.

"There's Gray Area?"

Ironically, amid the overwhelming evidence of cultural injustice I witnessed while spending time with my grandparents, I also glimpsed hope for humanity. The summer my parents divorced, my mother decided to send my brothers and me to stay with my grandparents for the season.

However, during that summer, fate dealt an unexpected blow. Unbeknownst to me, a pandemic was sweeping the globe, and I unwittingly fell ill to its grasp. Each time I stayed with my grandparents seemed to coincide with some ailment, and this time was no exception. As my fever spiked to a dangerous level, particularly precarious for a child of my age, my grandparents rushed me to the emergency room.

By that point, I had developed a profound awareness of both the stark realities of racism and its more subtle, insidious forms. The nurse attending to me approached her duties with a clinical detachment, treating me as if I were nothing more than a bothersome chore—distant, stern, and commanding in her demeanor, especially during medical procedures. Already frightened by my illness and the absence of my parents or grandparents, I could not shake the overwhelming sense of alienation within the hospital environment. Surrounded by White individuals, I felt acutely aware of my own Blackness, compounded by the perceived disdain of the nurse toward attending to my needs.

However, as I awaited admission to my room, a sudden ray of hope pierced through my fear; after I had been admitted and it was time to go up to my room in this scary place, it was as if God sent an angel to calm my fear. A tall, muscular White man with fiery red hair and freckles approached the nurse attending to me, engaging her in conversation. It was clear they were discussing me, likely arranging for my transfer. Indeed, he was the transporter or nurse's aide tasked with escorting me. Though his appearance initially struck me as intimidating, with his imposing stature and visible tattoo—an unfamiliar concept I had only heard unsettling rumors about—he attempted to engage me in conversation, albeit to no avail. Sensing my fear, he returned to the nurse, commenting on my apprehensive state, noting that I was alone.

Returning to me, he made another attempt to ease my anxiety. Then he squatted next to me, seated in a wheelchair. He said, "Hey, look at this." He curled his arm, balled up his fist, and bore his tatted arm. Then, I could now see an image of a hula dancer on his forearm. When he flexed his arm, she would dance. His playful display elicited a chuckle from me, breaking the tension and allowing him to establish a connection. He maintained a comforting dialogue throughout the journey to my room, gradually easing my fears.

Upon arrival, however, my anxiety resurfaced as I faced the intimidating room and the unfamiliar oxygen tent that would be my bed. Attempting to assist me, the orderly noticed my reluctance to uncover my foot. Then the orderly said, "Okay, let us get you in bed.". I attempted to get out of the wheelchair, but he stopped me and said, "Hold on a minute; I will put you in bed." He attempted to untangle the blanket I was wrapped in when he noticed I would not allow him to uncover my foot. He asked why I was doing that, and I explained that I had always had an allergic rash on my foot, and it was ugly, and I did not want him to have to look at it. I was ashamed enough that this White man had to deal with me, and in my mind, I thought he had to hate me for having to do this. Nevertheless, in a moment of profound kindness, he gently reassured me, dispelling my self-doubt with his words of acceptance. Scooping me up into his arms, he tenderly tucked me into bed, offering words of comfort before departing.

Alone and overwhelmed, tears welled in my eyes, but amid the turmoil, I found solace in the memory of this compassionate stranger. His act of kindness, a beacon of humanity in a moment of darkness, left an indelible mark on my soul.

Growing up and transitioning into adulthood, I grappled with the unsettling notion that people like me might forever be relegated to a lesser status solely because of the color of our skin. Despite my relentless efforts to defy this stereotype, it often felt like an uphill battle with little progress. Thankfully, along the way, I encountered individuals who embraced me for who I am. However, the pervasive sense of "us versus them," where "us" represented Blacks and "them" represented Whites, seemed insurmountable, leaving me to question if true equality would ever materialize within my lifetime.

It was not until my freshman year of college that I gained a deeper insight into the roots of this division. Enrolled as an art major, I found myself in a drawing class at a bustling state university. One particular day, the professor arranged the easels and stools in a large circle, deliberately positioning each student to draw the person directly in their line of sight. As I circulated to view everyone's work, I discovered I had unwittingly become the subject of many sketches.

One stood out among the approximately thirty portraits: a piece by another African American student that depicted my features precisely. The rest, however, fell victim to stereotypes, with exaggerated lips and a broad nose, distorting my likeness. It was a stark reminder that many could not see beyond preconceived notions of Blackness. In that moment, I felt reduced to a mere archetype, reinforcing the painful stereotype of being just another face in the crowd. It left me questioning if anyone could truly see me for who I am.

Ultimately, this experience has shaped my worldview, flawed though it may be. My perception is guided by what I have seen and experienced; "I see because I saw. Let me articulate the essence of this endeavor more effectively. For those fortunate enough to have traversed life without the weight of oppressive societal forces, I aim to broaden your empathy and ignite a sense of justice. Additionally, for those aspiring to aid in transforming individuals impacted by social injustices, this book offers a structured approach to providing support and fostering change.

Include Me, Not My Race

Throughout composing this book, I grappled with a recurring question: How do I authentically convey the profound personal significance of my experiences and captivate readers with my odyssey of confronting perceived injustices that have profoundly molded my life? I aspired to vividly portray how social injustices permeate the soul of an individual, potentially stifling their potential. I endeavored to spark a flame within readers, urging them to become catalysts for essential societal transformation, nurturing an environment where every individual can fully engage and flourish. If you were to ask, "Why does this matter to me?" I would respond that for a person to achieve full actualization, they must dare to confront and transcend their own self-interests, embracing a broader vision that encompasses the well-being of all.

One of the most poignant and compelling films I have ever watched is *To Sir, With Love*. This 1967 British drama, starring the legendary

Sidney Poitier, delves deeply into the social and racial issues faced in an inner-city school. Poitier, a Bahamian American actor, director, and diplomat, brings to life the character of Mark Thackeray, an engineer who takes up teaching in East London's North Quay Secondary School while searching for an engineering job.

North Quay is a tough school in a predominantly White neighborhood, where even the most troubled students are sent. The residents hold rigid views on race relations, often harboring prejudices against Black people. Thackeray's arrival as a Black teacher challenges these deeply ingrained biases. Through his compassionate and noble demeanor, he transforms the perspectives of both faculty and students. They learn to see beyond stereotypes and appreciate the shared humanity that binds us all.

The film is replete with compelling scenes, but one segment stands out, where Thackeray witnesses the profound impact of his inspirational approach and unwavering virtue. Thackeray, steadfast in his self-assurance and understanding of his worth, emerges as a beacon of change. One day before class, Seales, the sole Black student, confides in Thackeray about the recent passing of his mother. Deeply moved, Thackeray suggests that the class collect money for flowers to support Seales's family. However, when it comes to delivering the flowers and attending the funeral, Thackeray is disheartened to find that no student is willing to be publicly seen associated with Seales's family due to their race.

Throughout the film, Thackeray's antagonist, Denham—a young man embittered by life—relentlessly taunts him and seeks to undermine Thackeray's influence on the other students. Despite his disappointment in the students' response, Thackeray remains true to his character, maintaining his servant's heart toward them.

On the day of the funeral, there is a poignant scene where Thackeray, with flowers in hand, walks along the sidewalk toward the funeral procession. As he turns the corner, he is stopped by the sight of his entire class surrounding the hearse covered in flowers. He is amazed to see their normally unkempt faces now clean, well-groomed, and smiling, including Denham. They gaze back at their beloved teacher, who inspired them to rise above their biases and stand proudly with their classmate, demonstrating the love and unity Thackeray had instilled in them. His journey illustrates the profound impact one person can have in breaking down racial barriers and fostering mutual respect and love.

This film echoes my fervent plea, which I hope to leave as my legacy: to inspire us to look both within and beyond ourselves, to recognize and address the pervasive issue of bias. Unchecked prejudice stifles personal growth and limits opportunities for people to live freely and fully in the society they are born into. *To Sir, With Love* is a powerful reminder of the importance of confronting and overcoming these biases for the betterment of all.

I aim to extend a guiding hand to those who, like me, have faced similar challenges. While race serves as a focal point in this book, it is but one aspect of social injustice. By sharing my experiences, I aim to offer readers a glimpse into perspectives they may not have previously considered, urging them to be change agents and advocates for a more inclusive society.

For readers who have experienced life circumstances akin to mine, I encourage you to view the principles in this book as a source of guidance and support in transcending biases and cultural forces that inhibit your authentic expression. Transformation and personal growth are essential in breaking free from the shackles of injustice, influencing how we perceive ourselves and engage with others in diverse settings.

To those who wish to offer support and wisdom, this book serves as a beacon of enlightenment and empowerment. It is crucial to acknowledge that pursuing diversity, equity, and inclusion (DEI) initiatives is not merely a passing trend but a continuous journey toward creating a more just and equitable society.

Cultural intelligence catalyzes change and transformation, benefiting those who have experienced negative impacts and those who may be less affected. It encompasses recognizing and understanding cultural differences, including the norms, values, and beliefs that shape people's behaviors and perceptions.

An individual with high cultural intelligence possesses the skill to seamlessly adjust their communication style, body language, and approach to suit diverse cultural contexts. This proficiency fosters smooth and productive communication and collaboration across cultural boundaries. Furthermore, cultural intelligence equips individuals with the ability to navigate and resolve conflicts stemming from cultural misunderstandings or divergent viewpoints.

Those with cultural intelligence embrace interactions with individuals from diverse cultural backgrounds, viewing diversity as an opportunity for personal and professional growth. In essence, cultural intelligence empowers individuals to engage with the world in a manner that fosters empathy, understanding, and meaningful connections across cultural boundaries.

Darryl Washington, D.Ed.

ACUTE TRANSFORMATION

This work is about becoming culturally acute for those who have experienced bias and those who have been biased. The reader intending to consume this writing will potentially be transformed. Personal transformation is a deeply individual process involving significant internal shifts and growth. The transformation journey often begins with a moment of realization—a spark of self-awareness that reveals the need for change. This can stem from various experiences, whether overcoming adversity, experiencing failure, or simply feeling a sense of dissatisfaction with the status quo. From this initial recognition comes the desire for something different, the motivation to move beyond old patterns and embrace new ways of thinking, being, and interacting with the world.

An aspect of changing is letting go of the past and releasing old identities, relationships, or expectations holding a person back. It involves confronting fears, insecurities, and sometimes even grief over what is being left behind. Nevertheless, in letting go, space is created for new possibilities to emerge.

Understand there may be discomfort, but it will be worth it. Transformation does not happen in comfort zones; it requires stepping into the unknown, facing uncertainty, and taking risks. Whether trying new things, adopting new perspectives, or making difficult decisions, embracing discomfort is a necessary part of growth. You will become thick-skinned in the sense that you will develop resilience, as the journey of change is rarely linear and often filled with setbacks, challenges, and moments of doubt. Resilience is the ability to keep going despite these obstacles, learn from failures, and remain committed to the transformation process.

This may include adopting a growth mindset, where challenges are viewed as opportunities for learning rather than threats to one's identity. It may also involve developing greater self-compassion and understanding that growth takes time and that it's okay to make mistakes along the way. Personal transformation leads to authentic self-expression—a more authentic, confident, and aligned version of who a person is. This new sense of self often brings greater clarity, purpose, and fulfillment as the person begins to live in a way that reflects their deepest values and desires.

Personal transformation is about evolving into a more empowered, authentic, and resilient version of oneself. It is a process of shedding old layers, embracing growth, and stepping into a future that feels more aligned with oneself.

One of the key elements of personal transformation is self-reflection. To that end, after each chapter, there will be questions the reader is urged to consider so that transformation might begin. Change begins by looking inward and assessing one's thoughts, beliefs, and behaviors. This reflection allows for an honest evaluation of what is working and what is not, often uncovering deeply ingrained habits or mindsets that no longer serve a person's growth. I hope you enjoy the journey.

Reflection Questions

Chapter One

I. At what age do your earliest memories begin, and what stands out most from those early moments?

___

II. How do these early memories connect to developing your sense of self and identity over time?

___

III. Who or what significant events do you recall as having the most profound influence on shaping your identity?

___

CHAPTER TWO

BEING AND BELONGING

"To Whom Am I Belonging?"

Although it may not be common, I have vivid recollections from as early as two years old. Despite their diversity, these fragmented memories share a common thread: each represents a significant event that profoundly affected my emotions, often threatening my sense of self. Frequently, I felt like a mere observer, as if people, places, and things existed solely to be watched. In all my observations, I saw others as connected and belonging to one another. Nevertheless, I wondered what it takes to achieve that sense of connection.

Reflecting on my life, I am drawn to pondering the origins of consciousness, which seem intertwined with the fundamental question of selfhood. Do external factors define us, or do we shape our identities through our experiences and interpretations? Though often elusive, our earliest memories are the building blocks of our understanding and perception of the world. From these foundational moments, we construct our narratives, storing them in the repository of memory. While science explores the intricate workings of the brain, a conceptual exploration suffices to delve into the journey of self-discovery.

I now believe that my childhood experience of observing life is not unique but a path we all must walk as we make our initial discoveries about our existence. The most profound question we confront in life revolves around the quest for meaning or purpose. This pursuit is intrinsic to humanity, whether undertaken consciously or not, despite the inherent uncertainty it entails. Ultimately, we may all be searching for ways to connect or belong.

A sense of belonging has always eluded me. The yearning to fit in has been a persistent struggle from childhood through adulthood. Being acutely aware of cultural differences, especially regarding race, led me to believe that true belonging was unattainable. It seemed the general perception of me depended on conforming to a majority standard, one I knew I could never meet.

To the Victor, No Spoils

Reflecting on my fifth-grade class, I vividly remember when my Caucasian teacher, Ms. Farmer, announced a writing contest. The student who wrote the best story, as judged by her, would win a "prize." My friends, Doug and Aubrey, both White, were thrilled about the contest, and we were all eager to win. Most of the other kids in the class were African American, yet I struggled to connect with them. I did not feel out of place for not being "Black enough"; rather, I was drawn to things and people with different experiences. The other Afro-American boys talked about topics that did not interest me. Like Doug and Aubrey, I was not as into sports as they were; we could take it or leave it. At that age, boys and girls were naturally segregated, and boys deemed girls "cootie-infected." Regardless, the Afro-American never seemed to like me very much.

My teacher always seemed to favor Doug and Aubrey, and I thought it was because they were White like she was, while the classroom was otherwise all Afro-American students. My relationship with Doug and Aubrey was genuine, but I also believed that being friends with them was beneficial in gaining positive attention from Ms. Farmer.

The contest concluded, and I won with a story titled *Hair of Four Colors*. To my surprise, the entire class was happy for me and praised my effort. Ms. Farmer told me that her friend from the Lippincott Society said my book was publishable. I was overjoyed and proud; it felt like the most special thing ever happening. However, weeks went by, and I never received the promised prize.

Months later, my classmates rallied and confronted our teacher about her failure to deliver the promised prize for the best story. Annoyed, she went to the teachers' lounge, grabbed a dime candy, and dismissively declared it "the prize." Handing it to me with a look of irritation, she said, "Here." What should have been the pinnacle of my young life turned into a devastating disappointment. I could not help but wonder if Doug or Aubrey had won, would they have been celebrated more enthusiastically? Ms. Farmer seemed to favor them and enjoyed engaging with them. Despite always being with my friends, there was a noticeable difference in how she interacted with me. I suspected I was being slighted because I was not white, and this realization was deeply painful.

The prize I sought was not awarded for winning the book-writing contest. Instead, I yearned for approval and recognition, seeking affirmation and a sense of belonging. This contest was an opportunity to confront the lingering shame that had overshadowed me, a result of a lifetime of feeling inferior because I am a Black person. I believed winning the contest might open doors for deeper connection and acceptance, especially with Ms. Farmer. I hoped she would finally see me as an equal, like my friends Doug and Aubrey, and not through the lens of stereotypes that labeled me as inferior due to my race.

Truly Belonging?

Abraham Maslow, a renowned theorist and researcher, proposed that human needs are organized in order based on their predominance. This hierarchy is often depicted as a pyramid, each level representing a different needs category. According to Maslow's well-known and highly cited Hierarchy of Needs, the levels are as follows, in ascending order of prepotency:

1. Physiological Needs: These include basic survival requirements such as breathing, sleep, food, and water.
2. Safety and Security: These needs encompass physical health, a safe living environment, and essential resources. For children, this also includes having a reliable caregiver who ensures their health and meets their physiological requirements.
3. Love and Belonging: These fundamental human needs follow Physiological Needs and Safety and Security. They involve forming meaningful relationships and feeling a sense of connection with others.
4. Esteem: This need involves gaining respect and recognition from others and building self-esteem.
5. Self-actualization is realizing one's full potential and engaging in activities that lead to personal growth and fulfillment.

Maslow theorized that human motivation follows a pattern of deprivation, domination, gratification, and activation. This process continues until all the lower-level needs (physiological, safety, affiliation, and esteem) have been gratified, allowing the self-actualization need to be activated.

I encountered Maslow's work during my undergraduate studies, which resonated with me as a profound and fundamental truth. Growing up in an impoverished home marked by domestic violence, I felt light-years away from achieving self-actualization, the pinnacle of Maslow's hierarchy of needs. How could I aspire to reach the summit when my life experience had not transcended my belonging level? If society does not accept who you are, how can you ever become whole?

Although Maslow's construct has faced challenges and others have expanded upon his work, I found, as a former clinical psychologist, that his theories held essential truths. They illuminated the mental barriers in a person's life that significantly influence their basic motivations. People can become mired at any level of Maslow's hierarchy, living a life that never transcends basic needs. Concerning the lower levels of safety and belonging, I often wonder if a marginalized person can ever progress beyond this stage of development.

Wahba and Bridwell (1976) reviewed Maslow's concept of belonging and noted that his theory did not account for cultural differences between individualist and collectivist societies. They argued that these cultural variations can significantly influence how individuals prioritize their needs. In collectivist cultures, the emphasis is on community and altruism, whereas individualistic cultures focus on the rights and concerns of each person, promoting independence and personal identity.

However, cultural differences do not negate an individual's potential for transcendence within Maslow's hierarchy, designed to account for human development irrespective of social norms. Fundamental needs, such as safety, physiological well-being, and a sense of belonging, are universal. Achieving self-actualization may mean fulfilling the ideal of either a collectivist or an individualist mindset.

Also, studying Maslow's upbringing gave me a clearer understanding of his perspective. It appears that Maslow was primarily focused on human development rather than the potential effects of cultural differences. He was likely aware of these differences, particularly given his reported disdain for his mother's apparent prejudice against African Americans.

Maslow was born in 1908 and grew up in Brooklyn, New York, as the oldest of seven children. His parents were first-generation Jewish immigrants from Kyiv, then part of the Russian Empire. The family fled Czarist persecution in the early 20th century. Maslow's childhood was marked by encounters with antisemitic gangs who abused him by throwing rocks at him. He, along with other children in similar circumstances, struggled to overcome such acts of racism and ethnic prejudice. Given these experiences, Maslow likely had a substantial understanding of cultural differences.

Ravilochan (2021) uncovered unpublished papers by Maslow, revealing that his Hierarchy of Needs might have been influenced by the Siksika (Blackfoot) way of life. Maslow spent six weeks living among the Blackfoot people, which led him to reconsider some of his hypotheses about the Hierarchy of Needs. Initially focused on American narratives, Maslow's perspective shifted to incorporate the Blackfoot community's values.

FINDING CULTURAL ACUITY

Maslow aimed to test the universality of his theory that social hierarchies are maintained by dominance. However, among the Blackfoot, he did not observe the quest for dominance prevalent in mainstream American culture. Instead, he found a society characterized by cooperation, minimal inequality, restorative justice, well-nourished individuals, and high levels of life satisfaction. For the Blackfoot, the pinnacle of Maslow's pyramid—self-actualization—was a norm, with every individual seen as fully developed.

Maslow assessed the most successful individuals in the tribe to understand the difference between Blackfoot culture and his own. He discovered that wealth was not measured by money and property but by generosity. The wealthiest members had the least but gave the most, gaining true prestige and security through generosity.

Unlike Maslow's codified model, the Blackfoot did not have a formal framework for their worldview. Maslow viewed self-actualization as something to earn, while the Blackfoot saw it as innate. This perspective involved trusting people to express their inherent wisdom and granting them space to be themselves, as reflected in the permissive way they raised their children.

Maslow witnessed in the Blackfoot Giveaway that many First Nation cultures view meeting basic needs, ensuring safety, and creating conditions for expressing purpose as a community responsibility rather than an individual one. Blackstock refers to this as "Community Actualization." The skills to nourish a community-wide family, live in harmony with the land, and minimize conflicts are passed down through generations in First Nations communities. Each generation sees it as their duty to perpetuate their culture by adding to communal wisdom and teaching ancestral knowledge to their children and grandchildren. Despite these profound discoveries, Maslow did not share the insights or worldview of the Blackfoot people. It is believed that he feared losing his position if he elevated Siksika's teachings, as this might have undermined the validity of his ideas.

Culture is just one facet of a person's overall experience in developing a self-concept or identity. In my own experience, particularly with my mother, the development of self began within the nucleus of my immediate family and extended to interactions with extended family and the broader community. Maslow's concept of belonging focused on the basic human need for connection across various aspects of life, including family, work relationships, and other life encounters. My cultural experience shapes my need for belonging; I feel a sense of belonging is affected when my "Blackness" is seen as a factor in any given relationship.

The deeper need for belonging involves cultivating a connection with humanity and the individuals we encounter in various settings. Simmel and Elias (May 2011) suggested that belonging is the critical link between the self and society. However, fulfilling this need becomes challenging when most encounters are met with negative perspectives or value judgments. In such cases, overcoming the effects of bias in the broader community becomes essential. While one may achieve a degree of belonging within close familial relationships, attaining a profound sense of belonging from a cultural perspective may remain elusive.

"Belonging is not just about connecting with others; it also encompasses a sense of place, power, and purpose. The experience of belonging involves connectedness through community, rootedness in place, a feeling of ownership in shared outcomes, and a sense of mission with others" (Samuel, *The New Psychology of Belonging*, 2023). Purpose is closely tied to identity, but much of who we are is influenced by those we encounter and the context in which we meet them.

I attended a large state university with a diverse student body for my undergraduate degree, although the faculty was predominantly Caucasian or, in some cases, foreign nationals. For my master's degree, I attended a historically Black state university in a more rural community. My sense of belonging differed vastly between these experiences. At the predominantly Black university, I felt an inherent sense of belonging and needed to be less pretentious, without the constant worry of not measuring up or being enough. Conversely, during my undergraduate studies, I often felt inadequate, never smart enough, and out of place socioeconomically.

Maslow identified that our need for belonging is fulfilled through forming meaningful relationships and connecting with others. However, is one or more stable relationships truly satisfying this need? Belonging often seems more contextual or circumstantial, influenced by the environments we find ourselves in.

One of my few memorable high school experiences occurred during a class trip to New York with my merchandising class to explore the fashion industry. This trip was significant for me, as it was the first one I had funded myself, offering a newfound sense of independence. Despite the excitement of this liberating adventure, I felt profoundly alone. Being socially awkward, solitude was not unfamiliar, but this trip amplified my sense of isolation. None of my classmates were friends, and I had no real friends at school.

The experience was particularly challenging when we had free time for activities like shopping. Despite the captivating sights and sounds of New York, I realized that no one was concerned about me.

I felt disconnected and vulnerable, not knowing what to do or where to go if I got lost.

The situation worsened when my "forced choice" roommates violated a strict rule set by our teachers: males and females were not allowed to enter each other's rooms. One evening, a group of girls entered our room, and it became clear they had planned this activity. I distinctly remember hearing someone claim, "Darryl is mine." Uncomfortable and alarmed, I fled the room and reported the incident to our teachers and chaperones. As a result, my already low popularity plummeted further, and I found myself in an even more austere situation. I had never felt more out of place, starkly aware that I did not belong.

Belonging: Who Decides?

The concept of belonging, as discussed in the literature, often feels insufficient to me. Although various strategies and findings are presented, I remain skeptical about how much others can truly shape our sense of belonging. I believe that belonging is something we achieve when we decide we belong. It is a feeling of comfort and authenticity that goes beyond the need to modify ourselves for acceptance. True belonging allows us to be our genuine selves.

As Brené Brown wisely noted, "Fitting in is about assessing a situation and becoming who you need to be to be accepted. Belonging, on the other hand, does not require us to change who we are; it requires us to be who we are" (Brown, 2012, p. 145). Ultimately, we determine how to react to others' engagement, what values to embrace, and how to interpret social norms, customs, and traditions. Our responses become choices, especially as adults, while children, being more impressionable, might naturally conform more readily. What kind of learning experience empowers us to transcend reliance on others as gatekeepers of our sense of belonging?

According to Maslow's Hierarchy of Needs, our basic needs must first be met to create a foundation where people feel safe, respected, and comfortable being themselves. This includes the freedom to express all aspects of their identity without fear of social reprisal. However, when we are children, our most basic physiological and safety needs largely depend on others. This dependence trains us to look outwardly to meet our needs.

As we grow and develop the ability to fulfill our needs, we elevate to belonging. At this point, we attain greater stability and confidence by shifting our reliance from external validation to an internal sense of belonging. This involves not depending on others to define how we should belong or what is necessary to feel accepted. Additionally, belonging is intertwined with everyday practices often taken for granted and performed unconsciously, yet it also evolves dynamically over time and space. Therefore, belonging is "something we must continuously achieve through an active process" (Simmel and Elias, May 2011).

For instance, I cherished my friendship with Doug and Aubrey because they imposed no requirements on our relationship. Our shared traits, likes, and dislikes made fitting in and feeling a sense of belonging effortless. Conversely, with the other boys, there was a standard to meet—such as an enthusiasm for sports and roughhousing. I chose not to pursue their friendship because they could not dictate my sense of belonging. Learning to belong and being satisfied with this need is a process that could take a lifetime. It requires awareness and intentionality, as it is not the natural course of life. This journey involves recognizing and fulfilling our needs for belonging without relying on others to validate us.

"Othered, Then Belonging"

There is an American idiom known as the duck test: "If it looks like a duck, swims like a duck, and quacks like a duck, then it probably is a duck." Throughout my life, I have felt compelled to resist any aspects of my identity that aligned with stereotypes labeling me as Black. Regardless of how I presented myself, I was always perceived as a duck, irrespective of my actions or behavior. This was not due to self-loathing but rather a deep frustration and anger at being viewed through a racial lens instead of as an individual.

Escaping this scrutiny seemed impossible in a society that judges based on phenotype, heritage, language, and religion. The need to belong is shaped by larger sociological forces that push individuals to conform to cultural values. This lack of belonging hindered my ability to participate in life fully. Perhaps the most troubling thought is that, if I could, I would hide my identity as a Black man. I have long dreamed of a life where I would not be judged by my skin tone or surname, yearning for freedom from such prejudices. I often think about the countless times I have heard someone recount an event and say, "A black guy was there," even when the person's ethnicity had no relevance to the story. In the United States, people are so accustomed to putting race at the forefront of any statement that they rarely stop to consider its relevance. I also reflect on the myriad instances where I have filled out forms or encountered situations requiring me to indicate that I am black, whether I chose to identify as such.

For example, my wife is Caucasian, yet all our children's birth records classify them as Black, even though I never provided that information. The notion that someone is considered of African heritage simply because they have "a drop of Black blood" is both outdated and nonsensical. This pervasive emphasis on race, regardless of its actual relevance, highlights the deeply ingrained and often arbitrary ways in which racial identity is imposed and maintained in society.

Akbulut and Razum (2022) describe the concept of othering as a mechanism that delineates who belongs to a group and who does not. They explain that othering extends beyond simple discrimination based on categorization, highlighting its analytical capacity to capture the complex interconnections among knowledge structures, power relations, and categorization processes, thereby revealing their multifaceted impacts. Othering can uncover and highlight power dynamics in their intersectional forms, making these relations more accessible and visible. This analytical framework helps us understand how deeply embedded biases shape interactions and influence societal structures on multiple levels.

Akbulut and Razum (2022) explore othering as a discursive practice that operates on multiple levels, generating knowledge about who does and does not belong. This process renders certain groups socially visible as the other, distinct from a perceived we, thereby creating and sustaining a dominant relationship between non-others and others. This leads to inequality across various dimensions, including intersectionality, influencing research and care for minorities by embedding premises, ascriptions, expectations, and notions of normality that are difficult to recognize because they are seen as the norm. Consequently, intervention concepts advocating for inclusion and diversity are crucial for fostering social openness.

One of the most profound insights from the social and behavioral sciences is the persistent nature of the ingroup/outgroup effect (Billig Tajfel, 1973). This effect highlights our tendency to treat individuals within our perceived group more favorably compared to those we view as outsiders. While this phenomenon is evident in ethnic and religious contexts, it extends beyond these categories. The ingroup/outgroup dynamic is a fundamental aspect of human behavior, manifesting in virtually any context where people divide themselves into social groups. Whether based on nationality, political affiliation, profession, or even hobbies, the tendency to favor those within our own group while viewing others with suspicion or indifference is a universal pattern that shapes our interactions and perceptions.

Despite efforts to promote equity and inclusivity, the distinction between groups often persists, even under the guise of acceptance. We must examine our methods critically to foster inclusiveness and create spaces where everyone belongs. Health equity is a pertinent example, where institutions routinely collect data on race, assuming ethnicity significantly influences the incidence of certain illnesses within specific groups. However, the evidence supporting this approach is often weak, particularly concerning African Americans.

According to Bentley-Edwards et al. (2022), researchers and institutions increasingly align with anti-racism values and strive for more equitable research environments and practices. However, many remain uncertain about achieving these equitable ideals, leading to misperceptions that equity-related challenges are insurmountable. The framework proposed by Bentley-Edwards et al. (2022) emphasizes the need for a proactive and strategic approach to equity in research, which is integral to scholarly rigor and ethical practice. For example, many individuals classified as African American may have diverse genetic backgrounds, including significant European ancestry. In the absence of comprehensive DNA sequencing data, categorizing individuals solely based on race is illogical and potentially misleading. Someone with 40 percent European heritage, for instance, may not necessarily be predisposed to illnesses commonly associated with people of African descent. This underscores the need for more nuanced approaches that consider the complex genetic makeup of individuals rather than relying on simplistic racial classifications.

Achieving equity in research necessitates deeply recognizing the historical contexts that have shaped today's disparities. It involves integrating principles of anti-racism, antibias, and equity at every stage of the research process. This comprehensive approach encompasses the formation of research teams, the engagement of community wisdom and partnerships, the selection of research questions, the development of study designs, the execution of analyses, the interpretation of results, and the dissemination of findings (Bentley-Edwards et al., 2022).

Providing researchers with the tools to apply a racial equity lens at every stage of the research process is an urgent and critical task driven by ethical responsibility, the demand for scholarly rigor, and the increasing availability of equity-focused funding opportunities. This framework is designed to address structural, institutional, and interpersonal racism within research, yet its application extends beyond these areas, proving valuable across various disciplines, settings, and marginalized groups. To advance equity and dismantle structural racism, researchers and institutions must champion racial equity, forge alliances with affected communities, challenge existing norms, and continually seek to improve their practices (Bentley-Edwards et al., 2022).

My journey of self-discovery and longing for belonging mirrors the experiences of every other human being. A healthy sense of belonging can lead to numerous positive life outcomes. At the same time, its absence can result in a lack of meaning and purpose, increased risk of mental and physical health issues, and reduced longevity (Allen et al., 2021). Belonging is a subjective feeling of deep connection with social groups, physical places, and personal and shared experiences, making it challenging to help others cultivate and attain it.

According to Allen et al. (2021), there is considerable debate surrounding belonging, how it should be measured, and how individuals can fulfill their need for belonging. This lack of consensus stems partly from the breadth and theoretical diversity within the belonging literature, with various scholars approaching the topic from different angles and limited integration of these perspectives. Consequently, there is a pressing need to consolidate these diverse viewpoints to understand better belonging as a construct, how it can be evaluated, and how it can be cultivated.

This narrative review addresses key issues in belonging research, synthesizing disparate perspectives and leveraging their strengths. We propose an integrative framework for understanding belonging and discuss its implications for future research and practice. Social, cultural, environmental, and geographical structures broadly define the self's orientation, shaping perceptions of acceptance, morality, and belonging or alienation (Allen, 2020). The sense of self emerges from dominant social and environmental contexts, reinforcing and challenging one's subjective sense of belonging. Belonging is influenced by people, objects, and experiences within the social milieu, dynamically interacting with an individual's character, experiences, culture, identity, and perceptions. In essence, belonging exists "because of and in connection with the systems in which we reside" (Kern et al., 2020, p. 709).

With some exceptions, most people can develop skills to improve their ability to connect with people, things, and places. Social skills include awareness of oneself and others, emotional and behavior regulation, verbal and nonverbal communication, acknowledgment and alignment with social norms, and active listening (Blackhart et al., 2011). Cultural skills include understanding one's heritage, mindful acknowledgment of place, and alignment with relevant values. Social, emotional, and cultural competencies complement and reinforce one another, contribute to, and are reinforced by feeling a sense of belonging. For example, the ability to regulate emotions may reduce the likelihood of social rejection or ostracization from others (Harrist & Bradley, 2002). Competencies can also help individuals cope effectively with feelings of not belonging when they arise (Frydenberg et al., 2009). Pointing to the social nature of competencies, the display and use of skills may be socially reinforced through acceptance and inclusion, while feeling a sense of belonging may also assist in using socially appropriate skills (Blackhart et al., 2011).

As technology advances, the pace of modern life accelerates, traditional social structures erode, and cultural and ethnic values face increasing threats, heightening the need to help individuals establish and maintain a fundamental sense of belonging (Allen et al. 2021). By concentrating on competencies, opportunities, motivations, and perceptions, we can develop effective strategies to enhance the sense of belonging at both individual and collective levels. However, substantial effort and dedication are required to harness this framework's potential to benefit society fully.

Belonging appears to be a crucial factor in achieving cultural understanding. Cultural forces greatly influence how much a person feels they belong. Those who maintain a strong sense of belonging have a clear sense of self, determining their place independently of societal pressures to conform to expected norms. For those with cultural acuity, navigating cultural contexts involves a deep awareness and sensitivity to different cultures' nuances, customs, values, and behaviors, respecting these aspects while staying true to their own identity.

Reflection Questions
Chapter Two

I. Where do you see yourself most consistently positioned on the pyramid of belonging?

II. What factors have the greatest influence on your sense of belonging?

III. How do external relationships and personal experiences shape your sense of belonging?

CHAPTER THREE

PSYCHOLOGY IS TO CHICKEN AS CULTURE IS TO EGG

False Assertions Entrap People

For as long as I can remember, I have been drawn to the water, not just as a place to be but as something that feels almost essential—like a part of me. The idea of being submerged, cradled by its fluid embrace, captivates me in a way I cannot fully explain. It is as if, in those moments, the water becomes the air I breathe, and everything else fades away. The mere thought of it stirs something deep inside me, soothing the restlessness in my mind and body. There is a peace in that thought—a quiet, profound calm that washes over me, even when I'm far from shore. My yearning is not limited to being in the water itself. Just being near it, hearing the rhythmic lull of waves, or catching a glimpse of its endless expanse has always brought me a sense of tranquility that nothing else quite can. Therefore, learning to swim has long been a passion, a dream that I held onto fiercely.

I remember watching friends glide effortlessly through local pools, their laughter echoing as they splashed and played, and I felt a pang of envy. Some had pools in their backyards, and others shared stories of swimming in lakes or the ocean, stories that seemed to belong to a world just out of my reach. I would sit by the edge, feet dangling in the water, wishing I could be like them—free, weightless, one with the water.

But life has a way of keeping such dreams at bay. I never had the chance to learn, and when the opportunity finally came, I discovered that my body did not seem to take to the water as I had imagined. Floating did not come naturally. I remember one of my earliest attempts, filled with excitement and trepidation, where I was led to the deep end of a pool. They handed me a life jacket and urged me to jump in, assuring me that I would float. But to my utter dismay, I sank—life jacket and all. As I drifted helplessly to the bottom, panic set in, and I had to be pulled up by a lifeguard. The embarrassment stung as much as the cold water did, yet my love for water never faltered.

This passion for the water seemed almost irrational for someone who prides themselves on being thoughtful and rational, always looking before leaping. It defied my cautious nature. Nevertheless, one of my most cherished memories comes from that very passion—my first trip to the beach. My family was headed to Atlantic City, farther from home than I had ever been. I could not contain my excitement when we set off in the car. My mind was already in the ocean, imagining the feel of the waves against my skin. I must have asked, "Are we there yet?" more times than my parents could tolerate, but I did not care—I just wanted to see it, to feel it.

I will never forget when my dad turned the corner at the end of a long street, and there it was—the ocean. It stretched beyond me, vast and shimmering, a horizon that seemed to go on forever. It was unlike anything I had ever seen, and I was awestruck. To my young eyes, it was one of the world's greatest wonders, more glorious than anything I had ever imagined. At that moment, standing on the edge of the world, I felt like I had found something I had been searching for my entire life. The ocean was not just water—freedom, possibility, and an unspoken promise of adventure.

At six years old, I did not know how to swim and had no concept. I could barely slip off my trousers and shirt before racing to the water's edge and plunging in headfirst. The tide was coming in, and I was immediately swept up in a massive wave. It was a transcendent experience, a moment of stillness where time seemed to stand still, leaving me in awe, fascinated, and joyful. It was also the first time I nearly drowned, but I did not panic. Somehow, I managed to get to shore, and after coughing up the water in my lungs and clearing the remainder from my nostrils, I turned around and dove right back in.

Years later, in middle school, I had my first opportunity to swim in a pool, although I was supposed to stay in the shallow end. The moment we entered the pool area, I dove in headfirst and promptly began to drown, having misjudged the depth at just over five feet. I struggled to the three-foot section, coughed up the water in my lungs, and then returned to the deeper area.

This love for water, a bond I nurtured despite near-drowning experiences, became more than a personal passion. It turned into a quiet rebellion against the stereotype that Black people are "afraid of the water and cannot swim." For me, this stereotype is not just a lie about my own life but an unjust label imposed on countless other Black

FINDING CULTURAL ACUITY

individuals. What grieves me more is the collective burden this stereotype places on all Black people, as though it were yet another badge of shame society insists we wear.

This stereotype, like many, has deep historical roots. Some trace its origins to generational trauma passed down from the days of the trans-Atlantic slave trade, where an estimated ten to twelve million Africans were enslaved and transported to the Americas. Then, of course, there is the long, painful history of segregation that denied Black people access to pools, forcing them into substandard, unhygienic, and often unsafe swimming environments. The fear of water, for some, is not just a personal phobia; it is an inherited trauma compounded by systemic exclusion and discrimination.

However, the issue is not just historical. Cultural stereotypes continue to perpetuate these fears, with devastating psychological effects. The stereotype that Black people are afraid of water is not only false but also deeply damaging. Its origins lie in a combination of racist beliefs, cultural conditioning, and the systemic marginalization of Black people. Pools, symbolic of leisure and relaxation for some, were once battlegrounds for civil rights. Even years after the Civil Rights Act of 1964, segregation continued to thrive in public swimming pools.

This context is why Fred Rogers's simple yet radical gesture in 1969 resonates so profoundly. In an episode of *Mister Rogers' Neighborhood*, Rogers invited Officer Clemmons, a Black police officer played by François Clemmons, to join him in a small wading pool. The scene unfolded without fanfare—just two Black and White men cooling their feet together on a hot day. However, this seemingly mundane act shattered a racial barrier that existed in real life. Despite the Civil Rights Act, pools in 1969 still often shut out Black people, reinforcing the idea that Black bodies did not belong in these spaces.

Rogers, with his characteristic calm, defied this notion. When Clemmons said he did not have a towel, Rogers offered to share his own. At that moment, two men shared a pool and a towel—an unspoken yet powerful challenge to the bigotry that sought to keep them apart. Their casual intimacy, as simple as it seemed, was a profound statement against excluding Black citizens from swimming pools and, by extension, from society.

For François Clemmons, this scene was deeply meaningful. He later reflected on how it symbolized the hope that the world might change one day. Although that change is slow and ongoing, moments like this offered a glimpse of what could be—of a world where Black and White people could share not only water but a sense of belonging and equality.

The scene's impact lingered, leading Rogers and Clemmons to recreate it nearly twenty-five years later, this time with an even deeper gesture of kindness. When Clemmons appeared for the last time on the show in 1993, Rogers took the towel and dried Clemmons's feet, a gesture Clemmons likened to Jesus washing his disciples' feet. This intimate and personal act was not just about friendship but about dismantling the stereotypes and systemic barriers that had kept people apart for so long.

As I reflect on my experiences with water, I realize how this stereotype—like the one Fred Rogers quietly confronted—continues to permeate society. For me, swimming has always been an act of defiance, not just against the elements but against a narrative that would seek to diminish who I am. To love water, to submerge myself in it, is to reclaim something that was never meant to be denied to me or any of us. Like those in Rogers's wading pool, the ripples of change may start small, but they reach far, shifting the tides of history itself.

You Bias Me, I Bias You

Bias often manifests as stereotypes about individuals based on their membership in certain groups or inherent physical traits like gender, ethnicity, or sexual orientation. Such biases can lead to negative real-world consequences, whether consciously acknowledged or not. People may be unaware that they harbor these biases.

Reflecting on cultural stereotyping makes me ponder the extent to which our internalized thought processes and external cultural influences stigmatize us. It is a classic "chicken or the egg" dilemma: Which came first, our psychology or the influence of our culture? Reihl et al. (2015) categorize stigma as external and internal. External stigma, or public stigma, manifests as negative beliefs or attitudes (biases) that the general population holds about individuals identified as members of a stigmatized group. Internal stigma, or self-stigma, arises when individuals internalize these external biases, believing them to be true about themselves.

Explicit attitudes and biases are within our conscious awareness, allowing for reflection and self-monitoring. In contrast, implicit attitudes and biases are unconscious and automatically activated, often predicting behaviors more accurately than consciously held beliefs (Reihl et al., 2015). This dichotomy between explicit and implicit biases highlights the profound impact of internal and external influences on our perceptions and actions. By understanding the origins and mechanisms of stereotypes, we can begin to dismantle them, fostering a more inclusive and equitable society.

It might seem that external influences are the primary drivers of bias internalization, but inherent aspects of our cognitive architecture may also predispose us to subconscious bias. This suggests that bias can stem as much from nature as from nurture. In many ways, bias is adaptive, enabling us to use prior knowledge and experiences to inform our decisions and actions. This adaptive quality of bias facilitates more efficient information processing, allowing us to navigate complex environments more easily. However, while useful, our knowledge and experiences must be well-informed to ensure our biases are not negatively skewed. Not all biases are constructive and can, when left unconstrained, lead to poor decision-making.

According to De Martino (2006), framing bias occurs because people use their emotions to help make decisions. From an evolutionary perspective, this emotional input can be beneficial, as it often carries important information. Ignoring these emotional cues might mean missing out on subtle social signals that aid in making better decisions in various situations. However, in contemporary society, many decisions require abstract thinking and the ability to ignore irrelevant details, which may lead to relying on these emotional cues, sometimes leading to irrational choices.

Unconscious bias is our brain's instinctive shield against potential threats, intricately tied to our primal survival mechanisms. It swiftly categories and assigns labels to people and situations, expediting our decision-making processes. The amygdala, pivotal in processing emotions, particularly in triggering emotional responses, plays a central role here. When the brain detects a perceived threat, the thalamus swiftly relays sensory information to the amygdala, creating a cascade of fear responses. This activation triggers the sympathetic nervous system, initiating the fight-or-flight reaction. However, this rapid cognitive processing is not infallible and can lead to hasty judgments and misconceptions about others, with profound real-world implications.

Human brains are inherently predictive, shaped by past experiences that form expectations. This predictive mechanism optimizes cognitive efficiency by leveraging prior probabilities, minimizing the cognitive load of treating each new encounter as entirely novel. While primarily explored in basic object perception, Clark (2013) argues its applicability extends to social perception, a concept further explored by Otten et al. (2017). Clark (2014) posits that perceiving essentially involves predicting outcomes based on learned patterns and prior knowledge.

In a study aimed at understanding how the brain manages negative biases toward stigmatized groups, Krendl et al. (2012) uncovered two key findings. First, when participants tried to regulate their negative emotions toward stigmatized individuals, there was heightened activity in brain regions linked to emotion regulation, such as the anterior cingulate cortex (ACC) and the prefrontal cortex (PFC). This heightened activity suggests that stigma regulation requires significant cognitive effort initially. Second, the duration of this brain activity differed; stigma regulation was immediate, while general emotion regulation was sustained over time. This indicates that combating bias involves quick judgments, and reducing these biases requires deliberate, conscious effort.

Precursors to Bias: Understanding the Subconscious Forces Shaping Our Perceptions

Beneath the surface of our conscious awareness, the human brain operates with astonishing efficiency, processing vast amounts of information every moment. These processes are automatic, guiding decisions and judgments without explicit control. This rapid, unconscious processing is beneficial for navigating a complex world, but it also sets the stage for biases that are difficult to recognize and even harder to change. Understanding these brain mechanisms is essential to mitigate prejudice and foster healthier intergroup relationships.

One of the most fundamental cognitive functions contributing to bias is categorization. Our brains are wired to organize the world by sorting people into groups based on observable traits like race, gender, and age. While this process enables quick judgments, it can also lead to oversimplifications and the formation of stereotypes. As Perdue et al. (1990) point out, categorization naturally leads to the creation of "in-groups" (those we identify with) and "out-groups" (those we see as different), fostering favoritism toward our group and discrimination against others. These biases operate beneath the surface of our awareness, shaping our attitudes and behaviors in ways we may not fully realize.

In the intricate web of cognition, associations further reinforce bias. Hinton (2017) argued that these associations are not born from an innate cognitive defect but rather from the brain's predictive nature. Over time, cultural influences and personal experiences shape how we link certain traits with specific social groups. This process, often called "culture in mind," reveals how deeply embedded societal narratives influence our unconscious judgments. Importantly, implicit biases evolve alongside cultural shifts, though this change can be slow. Recognizing the role of culture in shaping cognition helps us see that these associations are malleable, but only when we understand the broader cultural context from which they emerge.

Another key cognitive mechanism that drives bias is selective attention—the brain's ability to focus on certain stimuli while filtering out others. While critical to our survival, this function also reinforces biases by causing us to pay attention to information that aligns with our existing beliefs while ignoring contradictory evidence. Johnston and Dark (1986) describe selective attention as the brain's way of filtering multiple sources of information, allowing us to tune into what seems most relevant—a picture attending a noisy industry conference, where dozens of conversations swirl around you. Amid the chaos, your brain zeroes in on a discussion directly related to your field, ignoring the background noise. This selective filtering shapes not just what we hear but also what we believe, as it allows biases to be reinforced when we focus on information that supports them.

Selective attention does not work alone—it interacts with emotional states and cognitive load. When we are anxious, our brains are more likely to focus on threats, contributing to what researchers call attentional bias. We may gravitate toward negative information in this state, reinforcing a skewed perception of reality. Similarly, those suffering from depression are prone to focus on negative stimuli, perpetuating cycles of bias and prejudice. When unchecked, selective attention strengthens confirmation bias, where individuals unconsciously seek out information that affirms their preexisting beliefs while disregarding alternative viewpoints. This tunnel vision prevents people from seeing the broader picture, making bias harder to identify and more challenging to dismantle.

Perhaps even more elusive than selective attention is the impact of implicit memory. Unlike conscious memory, implicit memory operates below the surface, subtly shaping our attitudes and decisions based on past experiences we might not even remember. Research shows that these unconscious memories reinforce stereotypes, particularly when it comes to race and gender (Sleek, 2018). For example, if someone frequently encounters members of a specific social group in stereotypical roles, these associations become ingrained, influencing future judgments and behaviors without conscious awareness. The fact that implicit memory operates automatically and without our awareness makes it a powerful, though often invisible, force in maintaining biases.

Implicit memory does not just recall past experiences but also affects mood and emotional states. Anxiety and depression, for instance, influence the way implicit memory functions, often amplifying negative associations. Someone experiencing anxiety may be more likely to remember threatening or harmful stimuli, thus perpetuating a biased worldview. This emotional distortion of memory further entrenches stereotypes as the brain unconsciously links negative traits with specific social groups. These biases are often so ingrained that individuals may not realize their discriminatory behaviors stem from implicit memories formed over time, shaped by societal norms, personal experiences, and cultural narratives.

The challenge in addressing these biases lies in recognizing them and confronting the deeply embedded mental processes that sustain them. As societal norms evolve—such as increasing acceptance of LGBTQ+ individuals or shifts in political landscapes—implicit biases may slowly adapt, but they are stubborn and resistant to change. While it is tempting to believe that education alone can eliminate bias, the reality is that these cognitive processes run deep. Only through continuous effort, both individually and collectively, can we hope to alter the course of these subconscious mechanisms.

In unraveling the intricate web of unconscious biases, we must consider the workings of the individual brain and the broader cultural and societal influences that shape these cognitive processes. Understanding the interplay between culture and cognition allows us to better recognize the origins of our biases and work toward a more equitable society where automatic categorization, selective attention, and implicit memory no longer serve as barriers to understanding and inclusion.

Bias by Reason

Leon Festinger, a pioneering figure in American social psychology, forever altered the landscape of understanding human behavior with his cognitive dissonance and social comparison theories. By daring to challenge the dominant behaviorist views of his era, Festinger illuminated the limitations of stimulus-response conditioning. He pushed the boundaries of psychological thought, advocating for a deeper appreciation of self-concept as a lens through which human actions could be understood. His legacy extends beyond these initial contributions, as his work sheds light on the complex interplay between cognition, social influence, and the biases shaping our world.

Cognitive dissonance is at the heart of Festinger's work, which occurs when an individual holds conflicting beliefs, values, or attitudes. This mental tension produces discomfort, prompting the person to seek resolution by altering their beliefs or justifying their actions to restore internal harmony. The theory strikes at the core of human decision-making, revealing why people are often reluctant to change their minds, even when faced with overwhelming evidence to the contrary. Festinger's insights into this psychological mechanism give us a window into how biases form and evolve.

Imagine the internal struggle of someone grappling with a long-held belief—perhaps about politics, religion, or social norms—who is confronted with evidence that challenges that view. The discomfort of dissonance is palpable, akin to a mental tug-of-war. Rather than simply changing their beliefs, many individuals seek refuge in bias as a coping mechanism, reaffirming their prior opinions and seeking information confirming them. This process is known as confirmation bias, where we unconsciously ignore evidence that contradicts our worldview, making it easier to maintain the comforting illusion of consistency.

Festinger's work in social communication and group dynamics further enhances our understanding of how bias operates individually and collectively. In 1950, Festinger introduced the proximity principle, which explores how physical and psychological closeness to others shapes our relationships. Proximity fosters connection; those who live, work, or study near us are more likely to become our friends and allies. In a landmark Massachusetts Institute of Technology study, Festinger found that students living in close quarters in the same dormitory were likelier to form strong friendships. The implications of this finding stretch far beyond dorm rooms; they suggest that the people around us exert a powerful, though often unnoticed, influence on our beliefs, behaviors, and biases.

The proximity principle can be likened to how we visually perceive the world. Just as objects close together appear to belong to the same group, we also tend to see those around us as part of our social "in-group." This clustering effect explains why we are often drawn to those who are geographically or psychologically close to us while viewing those outside our immediate circles with suspicion or indifference. Over time, repeated exposure to the same individuals strengthens these bonds, a phenomenon known as the mere exposure effect. It subtly shapes our biases, reinforcing preferences for the familiar while fostering unease about the unfamiliar.

The theory of informal social communication, another of Festinger's key contributions, delves deeper into the mechanisms that drive group cohesion. Festinger posited that individuals within groups experience a natural pressure toward uniformity—a force that compels them to align their beliefs and behaviors with the prevailing norms of the group. This pressure is strongest when individuals depend heavily on the group to meet goals or fulfill personal needs. In this dynamic, Festinger introduced the concept of perceived facilitation, the idea that uniformity within the group is not merely about fitting in but is essential to achieving shared objectives.

This insight offers profound implications for understanding how biases are reinforced within social contexts. The more dependent we are on a particular group, whether a professional circle, social network, or cultural community, the more likely we are to adopt the group's norms and values, even when they contradict our own. Festinger's research uncovers the invisible strings that bind us to group ideologies, pulling us toward conformity in ways that can both foster solidarity and perpetuate division.

In his social comparison theory, Festinger further elucidates how we define ourselves by looking outward to others. This natural human tendency to evaluate our abilities, opinions, and worth through comparison is a powerful force in shaping our self-concept. We constantly seek validation and understanding by measuring ourselves against those around us, striving to reduce uncertainty and solidify our place in the social hierarchy. Nevertheless, this comparison is a double-edged sword. While it can motivate growth and self-improvement, it can also lead to feelings of inadequacy, envy, and, in some cases, the birth of new biases.

As Festinger's work suggests, Biases are not formed in isolation—they are deeply embedded in our social and psychological fabric. They are the byproducts of cognitive dissonance, proximity, group dynamics, and social comparison, creating an intricate web of influences that shape how we see and judge the world. Nevertheless, these biases do not just distort our perceptions—they can also fuel more destructive emotions like hate.

Hate, much like bias, is both a psychological and social construct. It often stems from fear—the fear of the unknown, perceived threats, or loss of control. Through the lens of in-group and out-group distinctions, individuals find comfort in those they perceive as similar while casting suspicion or disdain on those they deem different. This categorization process simplifies the world and dehumanizes those outside one's social circle. Over time, these negative attitudes harden into prejudice and hate, perpetuated by socialization, cultural norms, and media narratives.

Festinger's theories, while not explicitly focused on the formation of bias, provide a robust framework for understanding how cognitive dissonance and social pressures can contribute to its growth. When confronted with new information or experiences that challenge our worldview, the discomfort of dissonance often drives us toward justifications that allow us to maintain our beliefs, even if they are flawed or harmful. These mental gymnastics preserve our internal harmony but at the cost of deepening our biases and, in some cases, reinforcing hate.

The human tendency to seek consistency, avoid discomfort, and align with the group is not inherently negative. However, these tendencies can lead us down dangerous paths without self-awareness and reflection, where biases go unchecked and hate festers. Festinger's work serves as a clarion call to examine the underlying mechanisms that drive our thoughts and actions. By recognizing the power of cognitive dissonance, proximity, and social comparison, we can begin to untangle the biases that cloud our judgment and work toward a more balanced and objective view of the world.

Ultimately, Festinger's theories remind us that while we may not always control the forces shaping our beliefs, we are responsible for how we respond to them. By fostering critical thinking, self-awareness, and open dialogue, we can mitigate the impact of bias and hate, creating pathways for personal growth and societal change. The journey toward overcoming bias begins with understanding its roots, and Festinger's work provides the road map.

Reflection Questions

Chapter Three

I. How do you think selective attention can contribute to developing or reinforcing biases, and what strategies can help mitigate this effect?

II. Can you recall when you experienced cognitive dissonance because you recognized your own bias? How did you handle the discomfort—did you try to justify your bias, or did it lead you to reconsider and shift toward a more unbiased perspective?

III. What will you do the next time you are exposed to unfair bias?

CHAPTER FOUR

"WHY CAN'T THEY SEE AS I SEE?"

I Am Black?

Honestly, I cannot pinpoint when I realized I was Black. Growing up, my mom, who appears Caucasian, looked like the other White people around us, and this made it hard for me to see my difference. It was not until I became more discerning and aware of social cues and the things people would say that I truly understood. My dad had his skin color, and my mom had hers, and I just thought this was merely a variation from one person to another.

Even when I learned about the differences of race, it was difficult to grasp why someone could treat me as less than because of it. Despite what I know today, it still seems baffling. I often think about how different my experience is from what my parents, grandparents, and Black ancestors endured. The Civil Rights Movement was well underway during my early years. Still, I can only imagine what it must have been like to be born into a time where, as soon as you had the cognitive maturity to understand, you knew you were Black and what that meant for your place in life.

My dad's parents were likely well-acquainted with "Remember your place," a saying deeply rooted in historical, societal hierarchies and power dynamics, embodying attitudes of superiority and subordination. This dynamic was palpably evident when I accompanied my grandparents on trips to town and observed their interactions with White people. At the time, I could not fully grasp the shift in their behavior in the presence of Whites, but in reflecting on it now, I would describe it as code-switching (Raddatz et al., 2023). However, it was not in the contemporary sense of the term that Black, Indigenous, and People of Color (BIPOC) code-switched to adapt their speech, appearance, and behavior to succeed in the marketplace. Code-switching aims to adjust one's style of speech, appearance, behavior, and expression in ways that will optimize the comfort of others in exchange for fair treatment, quality service, and employment opportunities (McCluney et al., 2019). For my grandparents, it seemed more like an attempt at survival by remembering their place, acting by the oppressive rules of Black codes and Jim Crow laws. Failing to abide by these rules and laws could be deadly.

Beginning in 1828, white actor Thomas Dartmouth Rice performed in blackface as a stereotyped character named Jim Crow, a routine that spawned numerous imitators. The term Jim Crow became a derogatory epithet for Blacks. Black codes were restrictive laws designed to limit African Americans' freedom and ensure their availability as a cheap labor force after slavery was abolished during the Civil War. Despite the Union victory granting freedom to some four million enslaved people, the status of freed Black individuals in the postwar South remained unresolved. Under Black codes, many states required Black people to sign yearly labor contracts; those who refused risked arrest, fines, and forced unpaid labor (History.com editors 2018).

Jim Crow laws were a collection of state and local statutes that institutionalized racial segregation for nearly a century, from the post–Civil War era until 1968. Named after a Black minstrel show character, these laws marginalized African Americans by denying them the right to vote, hold jobs, receive an education, and access other opportunities. Those who defied Jim Crow laws often faced severe consequences, including arrest, fines, jail sentences, violence, and death. States could authorize separate facilities for nearly every aspect of public life, including schools, hospitals, clinics, sports events, restaurants, barbershops, railroad and bus stations, restrooms, beaches, and public parks.

The Pain of Code-Switching

The behavioral adjustments my grandparents made in the presence of White people were a direct response to the oppressive laws and societal expectations of their time. Their code-switching served as a survival mechanism, enabling them to navigate and endure the deeply ingrained racial hierarchies. This adaptive behavior was not merely a personal choice but a reflection of the broader societal pressures and systemic racism that dictated their lives. They were always on guard, vacillating in and out of who they were in the very definition of themselves, never able to fully be present as an intact representation of the person they were and would like to be.

Assimilation of cultures does not necessarily erase or eradicate them but leaves those affected with the burden of suppressing their full identities. This often results in code-switching, a form of cultural suppression. The concept of code-switching continues to evolve in response to changing social constructs. Cultural code-switching involves concealing or altering aspects of one's cultural identity, such as clothing, hairstyle, speech, or behavior, to blend in with a dominant culture.

At its core, code-switching means adapting one's presentation to distance themselves from cultural or racial stereotypes associated with their group. This socially motivated strategy aims to produce a sequence of unmarked choices, ultimately establishing themselves as the marked choice. By doing so, individuals attempt to navigate social environments more successfully, often at the cost of their cultural authenticity. Code-switching is particularly relevant for individuals who identify as Black, Indigenous, or people of color (BIPOC), who often find it necessary to navigate professional settings effectively. It involves altering one's appearance or behavior to enhance the comfort of others, typically those outside their cultural or racial group, in hopes of receiving equal treatment and opportunities for advancement.

What if you had to decide daily whether your traditional cultural garments would be acceptable in your workplace or school? They might question if wearing a turban, hijab, or bindi will be off-putting to colleagues or supervisors or if their natural hair—an afro, dreadlocks, or braids—will be considered unprofessional. This constant negotiation of cultural identity highlights the broader impact of cultural suppression. Understanding code-switching within this broader historical context of cultural suppression reveals its implications. The practice of code-switching and the historical erasure of Indigenous cultures both illustrate how marginalized groups have been pressured to conform to the dominant culture, often at great personal and communal cost.

Adikwu (2020) emphasizes the mental health costs of code-switching, highlighting the physical and emotional toll it takes on individuals. The pressure to code-switch can be both physically and emotionally draining, causing individuals to feel as though they have lost their cultural identity or abandoned their heritage. Over time, the constant need to conform to a dominant culture can lead to burnout and emotional exhaustion.

Code-switching involves navigating assumptions about proper and informal dialogue, which can be perceived negatively due to the inconsistency of multiple meanings and connotations within a conversation. This inconsistency can make it challenging to understand when different dialects simultaneously convey a single thought, especially when context or syntax changes mid-conversation. Additionally, concealing aspects of one's identity to code-switch may result in negative feedback from those within one's cultural community, leading to accusations of "acting White." This can induce feelings of guilt and social withdrawal. Moreover, attempting to avoid or prevent stereotyping through code-switching can eventually lead to work performance issues. Symptoms of burnout from code-switching may include:
- Feeling detached from one's environment or reality
- Experiencing emotional exhaustion
- Feeling dissatisfied with one's life or job
- Suffering from irritability or extreme stress
- Exhibiting low performance at work or school
- Not feeling a sense of accomplishment

Essentially, it seems that there are potentially generations of people who have been culturally suppressed, may not have a real sense of belonging, or have identity confusion.

While each generation may influence the next, this does not necessarily silence the pervasive negative social norms and conventions. Roughly sixty years ago, President

Changelings

Lyndon B. Johnson signed the Civil Rights Act of 1964, a landmark legislation that aimed to transform the landscape of race and gender relations in American society. Despite the significant progress this law promised, the anticipated social change has not fully alleviated the struggles of Black Americans. Persistent and significant issues remain where Black people and other ethnic minorities continue to face cultural suppression and systemic discrimination.

I often wonder if social change can reliably bring effective help to marginalized individuals and those suffering from cultural bias. What must a social movement achieve to relieve those trapped in social and cultural dilemmas? Kavanagh et al. (2021) highlight that millennial Americans are not experiencing particularly rapid social change compared to 1900 to 1950. Their analysis suggests that social change does not occur in predictable, long, wave-like cycles. Rather, it follows a model of punctuated equilibrium, where periods of relative stability are interrupted by short bursts of significant change. This perspective underscores the complexity of social transformation and the ongoing challenges marginalized communities face in achieving true equality and justice.

If positively implemented, social change potentially effectively shapes the most important aspects of society. The force of the change that occurs is internal and external in places where we live, work, and interact. It is important to explore and examine what drives these changes and how societies adapt as we learn how dynamic our social world is. The future is fixed, and we have the opportunity to help shape and mold it through the actions and decisions of people.

When we talk about social change, we mean significant shifts in a society's structure, organization, and function. Our norms, values, laws, and institutions show these changes. They are not random; they have direction—either moving us forward or backward, affecting societies on multiple levels ("The Dynamics of Social Change: An Overview," Sociology Institute, 2023).

Internal forces, like innovation, ideological changes, and demographic shifts, play a big role in transforming societies from within. Technological advancements and fresh ideas can completely change how societies function. Think about how the Internet has revolutionized communication, commerce, and education. Ideological shifts, such as changes in collective beliefs and values, can lead to major social reforms. The Civil Rights Movement, for example, shows how changing ideologies can reshape laws and societal norms. Demographic shifts, including population size, age structure, and composition changes, also significantly impact social policies and economic conditions. Aging populations in many countries are prompting changes in health care and retirement systems.

External forces include environmental factors, economic interdependence, and cultural exchange. Natural disasters, climate change, and resource scarcity force societies to adapt, leading to new settlement patterns and economic practices. Global trade and financial markets create economic interdependence, making societies vulnerable to economic changes far beyond their borders. Cultural exchange, driven by migration, travel, and communication, spreads ideas that can spark change. The worldwide spread of democracy over the past century shows how cultural exchange can transform societies.

Research shows that many people prefer to remain bystanders rather than take action. Social movements like Black Lives Matter gain momentum when they receive widespread support for their social justice goals. These movements thrive when individuals unite in solidarity, sharing a mission to combat injustice and inequality (Nardini et al., 2020). Social change, therefore, occurs through the concerted efforts of individuals, organizations, and networks working toward a common cause.

Successful social movements mobilize diverse participants with various skills, abilities, and perspectives. A crucial challenge is transforming bystanders—those unaware of the issues or lacking motivation to act—into upstanders who actively contribute to solutions. Understanding what drives individuals to join collective action at the grassroots level and harnessing this momentum is key to creating lasting social change.

In their 2020 work, Nardini et al. suggest a unique lens through which to understand social change—by examining it from the perspective of consumer psychology. This shift in focus reframes social movements as collective, external efforts and as deeply personal transformations. At the heart of these movements are the choices and motivations of individuals, each driven by a blend of personal insight and shared purpose. When we think of consumer psychology, we often consider how people make purchasing decisions or engage with brands, but it goes far beyond that. It explores the full spectrum of human behavior—how people think, feel, and act. It delves into the cognitive and emotional triggers that push people to align with a cause, question their beliefs, or decide to stand up as upstanders rather than remain passive bystanders.

In this context, social change becomes a collective awakening, with consumer psychology offering valuable insight into the motivational and emotional currents that drive people to take action. It reveals how deeply intertwined personal identity, decision-making, and social movements are. By understanding these forces, we can see why some movements gain momentum while others falter. It's not just about rallying people to a cause; it's about tapping into the individual motivations and cognitive processes that compel them to invest in that cause, both emotionally and behaviorally. Social movements succeed when they resonate personally when individuals recognize themselves in the broader struggle and are moved to act in unison with others.

Social movements can address societal inequities through grassroots efforts influencing public policy and legislative changes. Overcoming systemic inequalities requires bottom-up organizing (Crutchfield, 2018; Meyer, 2015; Satell 2019). As Fredrick (2018) emphasized, people must believe that "Change is possible. Change is deliberate." Additionally, movements must connect, elevate, amplify, and empower business leaders, social entrepreneurs, and local leaders ready to be part of the solution (Friedman, 2020). Researchers must continue exploring the psychological processes that enable people to unite, build social movements, and collectively create a more just society.

Tracking social change from a sociological perspective can provide limited insights into its impact on affected groups, whether positive or negative. De la Sablonnière (2017) argues for a shift in focus; while sociological theories often explore the causes of social change, they frequently overlook its psychological consequences. De la Sablonnière's research emphasizes the need to examine the psychology of social change. In her 2017 study, 325 articles meeting strict inclusion criteria were analyzed to develop a new multilevel typology aimed at conceptualizing and categorizing social change based on its psychological impact on well-being. This typology identifies four social contexts: Stability, Inertia, Incremental Social Change, and Dynamic Social Change (DSC). DSC is characterized by four features: the pace of social change, disruption of social structures, disruption of normative structures, and level of threat to cultural identity. A theoretical model linking these characteristics to the social contexts is also proposed.

I find De la Sablonnière's thesis compelling because culture, or what some might call nurture, can profoundly shape our identity and ways of thinking, forming the very foundation of our worldview. Cultural psychology aims to offer a comprehensive understanding of human behavior by embedding cultural context into psychological research, illuminating human experiences' rich diversity, and challenging the assumption of universal psychological principles. This fascinating branch of psychology delves into how cultural contexts mold and influence human behavior, thoughts, emotions, and mental processes. It explores the profound impact of cultural traditions, social practices, and collective beliefs on individuals and groups and how these cultural elements interact with psychological functioning. For social change to positively impact societies, it must initiate transformation at the individual level, one member at a time.

"The Defiant Ones"

Sidney Poitier once declared, "I had no idea that my color, this color, is my color, not the condemnation of me." In this powerful statement, Poitier defies the condemnation—a harsh judgment or disapproval—that has long been a weapon of bias used against people of color and marginalized groups. His words were a bold defiance, rejecting the notion that he needed to conform to the low expectations set by others. Instead, he aimed to surpass these limiting beliefs. How did he remain undiminished in the face of those who viewed him as lesser? He did not recognize his color as a barrier, and thus, he remained unburdened by their prejudices.

There was a time in my innocence when I did not see color or race as an issue. My parents, one appearing as Black and the other as White, made the color of people a nonfactor for me. However, when I realized that a person's hue and appearance mattered to society, I felt confused, frustrated, and scared. It dawned on me that my skin color could condemn me and that the power dynamics in play left me feeling powerless, unable to rise above a position that felt inherently lowly.

Reflecting on that period, I adopted a passive-aggressive denial of my reality, unlike Sidney Poitier, who embodied defiance and grace. This denial only served to partially shield me from overwhelming feelings of insecurity, shame, and insignificance. How does one emerge defiant of their imposed perceptions in a culture that categorizes and ranks people as superior or inferior?

Sidney Poitier's story begins on Cat Island in the Bahamas, where his ancestors are believed to be migrants from Haiti. The Poitiers may have been among the runaway slaves who established maroon communities throughout the Bahamas, including Cat Island. Maroons, descendants of Africans in the Americas and the Indian Ocean islands who escaped slavery, formed their own settlements, often mixing with Indigenous peoples and evolving into unique Creole cultures. Like all the larger Bahamian islands, Cat Island was initially populated by Lucayan Indians until the Spanish arrived and took them into captivity as slaves. Cat Island is a quaint island and cultural hub in the Central Bahamas, rich in authentic Bahamian traditions and folklore.

Sidney was raised in the modest confines of a farming family, and from a young age, he intimately knew the sting of poverty. He wore clothing made from sacks and had little exposure to the finer things in life. His early years were marked by limited formal education, which, according to one documentarian, ended after the second grade. During his formative years, he lived in a world seemingly untouched by the outside world, reminiscent of the nineteenth century or earlier. In interviews, he recounted how, upon first seeing automobiles, he asked his mother, "What kind of beetles are those?"

At fifteen, Sidney was sent to live with his brother in Miami to stave off an inclination toward delinquency. There, he encountered the harsh reality of America's racial divide, a profound shock for a boy from a predominantly African-descended society. On one occasion, he was followed by police for fifteen blocks, who threatened to shoot him if he did not confront them.

At eighteen, Sidney's journey led him to the bustling streets of New York City. He persevered through menial jobs, sometimes finding shelter in the toilets of bus terminals. A brief stint in the army, working at a veterans' hospital, offered little respite from his struggles. Back in Harlem, he continued to toil in lowly jobs until a spur-of-the-moment audition at the American Negro Theatre changed his trajectory. Though initially rejected harshly, Sidney spent the next six months rigorously working on his accent and honing his acting skills. His unwavering determination paid off when he was finally accepted on his second attempt.

During a rehearsal, a casting agent noticed Sidney's potential, leading to a bit part in the Broadway production of *Lysistrata*. His performance garnered positive reviews, and by the end of 1949, he found himself at a crossroads, choosing between prominent stage roles and an offer from Darryl F. Zanuck to star in the film *No Way Out* (1950). His portrayal of a doctor treating a White bigot brought him significant attention and more roles, though these were often less substantial than those afforded to his White counterparts.

However, seven years later, Sidney's steadfast refusal to accept demeaning roles began to bear fruit. He landed a series of roles that elevated him to a status seldom reached by African-American men of that era: that of a leading man. One of these films, *The Defiant Ones* (1958), earned Sidney his first Academy Award nomination for Best Actor. In 1963, he made history by winning the Oscar for his performance in *Lilies of the Field*, becoming the first African American to win a leading role. His perseverance and unyielding commitment to his craft paved the way for his groundbreaking achievements and enduring legacy.

Classic Black versus Neo-Black

I am deeply fascinated by Sidney Poitier's story, as he rose above bias, racism, and bigotry. In Maslow's terms, he was a self-actualized individual, embodying the highest standards within himself, traditional and long-established in form and style. Despite the challenges of being

Black in American culture, he never seemed to relinquish the dignity that comes from a profound sense of self-worth. I believe this self-assurance was nurtured by his community on Cat Island, where limited diversity meant he was valued as a person, not judged by race or ethnicity by a larger majority ethnicity. His identity was not shaped by a society where race is a currency valued based on its denomination. I often wonder what I and others like me could have achieved without the limitation and burden of being judged by my skin color.

Sidney Poitier was spared the identity distortion that often plagued Black individuals shaped by the American culture of racial segregation. Many Black individuals from the Caribbean and Africa, in my experience, possess a sense of identity that remains intact, unfractured by the challenges of minority status. They originate from communities where African lineage is the norm rather than the exception. While they encounter systemic challenges in North American societies, they often exhibit greater resilience against racial stigmas and are more likely to reject narratives that deem them inferior.

In contrast, Black Americans frequently grapple with a self-concept forged within a culture that has historically been shaped by systemic racism and disadvantage. Born into more culturally cohesive environments, figures like Poitier often exhibit a more robust and grounded sense of identity. While Black Americans have long sought to preserve and connect with their heritage, the cultural conditioning they endure often requires a neoclassical effort—one that reconstructs a history detached by time and shaped by the adaptive demands of contemporary realities.

The 1977 television miniseries Roots, based on Alex Haley's novel *Roots: The Saga of an American Family*, ignited a profound cultural awakening for many Black Americans. It portrayed Haley's family's journey and brought the African American experience to life. For many, *Roots* served as a bridge to their African heritage, humanizing the narratives of enslavement and resistance. It emphasized the enduring traditions, language, and familial bonds that had survived centuries of dislocation and erasure. Beyond its emotional impact, the series inspired widespread genealogical research and sparked a surge of interest in African ancestry, prompting many to visit Africa in search of deeper connections. The miniseries cultivated cultural pride, empowering Black Americans to reclaim their heritage and reject the systemic erasure wrought by slavery and racism. Importantly, it also brought the realities of slavery into mainstream conversation, fostering a broader appreciation for African culture and the legacy of the transatlantic slave trade.

The movement among Black Americans to connect with African roots has deep historical foundations but gained significant momentum during the 20th century. During the antebellum period, some freed Black Americans—such as those involved in the American Colonization Society—sought to reestablish ties with Africa as part of a broader vision for freedom and self-determination, exemplified by the founding of Liberia in 1822. Later, the Harlem Renaissance of the 1920s marked a cultural flowering, during which African American intellectuals, writers, and artists began reclaiming African heritage as a source of pride and inspiration. Figures like Langston Hughes and Zora Neale Hurston infused their work with African cultural motifs, laying the groundwork for future reclamation efforts. Leaders like W.E.B. Du Bois and Marcus Garvey amplified this connection in the early 20th century. Garvey's "Back to Africa" movement emphasized Black pride and a return to African heritage, while Du Bois's advocacy for Pan-Africanism united the struggles of Black people worldwide.

The Civil Rights Movement of the 1950s and 1960s brought a renewed focus on African heritage as activists began openly rejecting Eurocentric standards of beauty and culture. The Black Power movement took this further, celebrating African heritage as a source of strength and pride. Organizations like the Black Panther Party promoted Afrocentric symbols and practices, while the 1970s ushered in a cultural renaissance. Afrocentric education, art, music, and fashion became widespread, with traditional African clothing like dashikis and natural hairstyles such as afros symbolizing a reclamation of identity. Modern movements continue this legacy, with African Americans engaging in genealogy and DNA testing and traveling to Africa to deepen their connection to their roots. Festivals like Kwanzaa, established in 1966, reflect a contemporary synthesis of African cultural values and Black American identity.

The journey to reclaim African heritage has profound implications for restoring dignity and identity among Black Americans. Understanding and celebrating their heritage provides a counter-narrative to the negative stereotypes that have long-defined perceptions of African descent. However, one must ask: Can this reclamation foster a strong sense of self for those who have been indoctrinated into a culture that has historically perpetuated their inferiority? While reconnecting with African roots offers a powerful means of cultural restoration, it remains an ongoing process to overcome the deep psychological scars of systemic racism and create a future where identity is not constrained by historical prejudice.

For Black individuals born in the United States, whose ancestors were often forcibly brought to the country through the chattel slavery trade rather than as immigrants, developing a strong sense of self can be particularly challenging. This struggle is intensified by a society that still reflects a lesser status for them. Jalata (2002) conducted a historical review that explored the difficulties and challenges Black Americans have faced in their quest for true freedom and self-identification. He concluded that the transformation of Black America has not been successful. According to Jalata, the majority of African Americans still lack meaningful access to the political, economic, and cultural resources of the country.

Although the African American movement introduced the agenda of multiculturalism, the struggle for cultural identity remains an unfulfilled aspiration. The suppression of revolutionary nationalism, the denial of self-determination for the Black community, and the imposition of order politics on the Black masses and revolutionaries perpetuate the underdevelopment of Black America. Change is thwarted by a vortex of social ills that ensnare a majority of African Americans, keeping them in substandard living conditions. These conditions include disproportionate cases of police brutality, low socioeconomic status, illiteracy, disease, unemployment, crime, drugs, and urban crises. This relentless cycle of adversity undermines efforts toward true liberation and equality, trapping many in an unending struggle for dignity and opportunity.

African Identity?

Regardless of race or ethnicity, we all desire to be included and accepted for who we truly are and aspire to be. This yearning for acceptance is universal, yet for those labeled as Black, African American, or African, the authenticity of this acceptance is often questioned. In the United States, the complexity of identity is profound, as almost no one can trace their ancestry to a single place.

A fascinating genetic study has revealed the surprising ancestry of many Americans. Researchers discovered that a significant percentage of African Americans, European Americans, and Latinos have a genetic heritage that extends beyond their self-identified ethnicity. For instance, the average African American genome is nearly a quarter European, while almost 4 percent of European Americans carry African ancestry. This highlights the intricate legacy of migrations and interactions over the past few centuries, clearly visible in the genetic makeup of modern Americans.

These findings suggest that genetic ancestry can augment historical records and shed light on the cultural processes shaping contemporary populations. The relationship between self-reported identity and genetic African ancestry, coupled with the low numbers of self-reported African Americans with minimal African ancestry, offers a deeper understanding of the complex interplay between genetics and social constructs of race. It also reflects the impact of racial categorization, assortative mating, and notions of race on patterns of mating and self-identity in the US.

Empirical evidence supports that over recent centuries, many individuals with partial African and Native American ancestry have "passed" into the White community. This is established by multiple lines of evidence showing African and Native American ancestry in self-reported European Americans. Although the majority of European Americans in the study did not carry Native American or African ancestry, the small proportion did translate into millions of individuals with such heritage. The early history of the US, starting in the seventeenth century, was likely a period of significant population interactions and admixture, contributing to today's rich and diverse genetic tapestry.

Unlike Sidney Poitier, who emerged from a homogenous community where every face mirrored his own, African Americans shape their identities within the vibrant mosaic of a multicultural society. Here, they frequently find themselves in the minority, navigating a rich tapestry woven from the intricate threads of psychological, social, and cultural influences.

Developing identity is a continuous and dynamic process. It involves navigating various psychological stages, cognitive developments, social interactions, and cultural contexts. By integrating insights from renowned theorists and recognizing the influence of family, peers, and life experiences, we understand how we come to know and define ourselves. Renowned theorists have illuminated this complex journey, offering profound insights into how we come to understand who we truly are. Erik Erikson, a pioneer in developmental psychology, envisioned identity formation as a voyage through eight stages of psychosocial development. Particularly during adolescence, in the stage he termed "Identity vs. Role Confusion," individuals grapple with questions of self, seeking to emerge with a clear and cohesive sense of identity. Successfully navigating this stage is akin to finding one's true north amid the swirling uncertainties of youth.

James Marcia expanded the metaphor of identity as a vast landscape where individuals embark on journeys of exploration and commitment. Within this dynamic terrain, they traverse periods of uncertainty and self-discovery, carving out unique paths that reflect their personal experiences and choices. Building on Erikson's foundational theories, Marcia delved deeper into the intricate process of identity formation, identifying four distinct statuses that illustrate the delicate balance between exploration and commitment.

The first status, **Identity Diffusion**, is characterized by a pervasive sense of confusion. Individuals in this stage find themselves adrift, lacking both exploration and commitment. They have yet to dive into the myriad options, leaving their sense of identity nebulous and undefined. In this phase, uncertainty reigns, and decisions about who they are remain tantalizingly out of reach.

Moving along the landscape, we encounter **Identity Foreclosure**. A commitment is present here, but it is built on the shaky foundation of others' influences rather than personal exploration. Individuals in this stage have settled on a specific identity, often shaped by family, peers, or societal expectations, without engaging in the critical questioning or investigation of alternatives. Their identity is like a structure erected without a solid plan, leaving little room for genuine self-discovery.

Next is the **Identity Moratorium**, a phase filled with vibrant exploration. Individuals in this status actively seek out experiences, experimenting with different roles and ideas as they navigate the labyrinth of possibilities. While deeply engaged in this process, they have not yet anchored themselves to a definitive identity. This stage is characterized by excitement and uncertainty as individuals embrace the freedom to explore without the pressure of immediate commitment.

Finally, we reach **Identity Achievement**, a stage representing the culmination of a thorough journey of self-exploration. Here, commitment follows a period of thoughtful consideration and discovery. Individuals emerge from their explorations with a well-defined and personally validated identity. They stand firm in understanding who they are, thoughtfully navigating the landscape of possibilities, and making choices that resonate with their authentic selves. In Marcia's rich framework, the landscape of identity is not just a place of passage but a vivid, evolving journey that invites individuals to engage deeply with themselves and the world around them.

Socialist theorists like Lev Vygotsky highlighted the importance of social interactions and cultural context in identity formation. Learning occurs within the "zone of proximal development," where guidance from more knowledgeable others helps individuals develop their self-concept. Albert Bandura's social learning theory added another layer, describing identity formation as a dynamic dance of observation and imitation. Bandura's theory suggests that identity is formed through observation, imitation, and modeling. The concept of self-efficacy, or the belief in one's ability to succeed, is crucial in shaping one's identity. In this dance, self-efficacy—the belief in one's abilities—is pivotal, empowering individuals to carve their paths.

Jean Piaget offered a different perspective, illustrating how cognitive development shapes our self-concept, much like a lens bringing the world into sharper focus. Piaget emphasized how cognitive development shapes our understanding of ourselves and the world. As children progress through stages of cognitive development, their ability to think abstractly and understand complex concepts, including identity, matures. Lev Vygotsky emphasized the role of social interactions and cultural context, portraying identity as a sculpture shaped in the zone of proximal development guided by mentors and peers.

George Herbert Mead's symbolic interactionism further enriched our understanding by highlighting how societal expectations and roles are internalized, much like a sculptor molding clay. Mead proposed that identity evolves from cultural influences where identity forms and is constructed through social interactions. The self emerges from the ability to take the perspective of others and internalize societal expectations and roles. This process underscores the profound impact of social interactions on our sense of self.

Another culturally derived perspective on identity formation comes from Henri Tajfel and John Turner, whose social identity theory highlights the powerful influence of group membership on identity. Their theory reveals that individuals derive a significant part of their self-concept from their communities, fostering a sense of belonging and distinctiveness. According to Tajfel and Turner, group membership shapes our perception of ourselves and others, providing a crucial foundation for our identity by offering a sense of inclusion and uniqueness.

These theorists vividly depict identity formation as a dynamic interplay of individual growth, social interactions, and cultural contexts. It is a journey through a richly textured landscape where every path taken and relationship formed contributes to the ever-evolving story of who we are.

Socialization plays a crucial role in shaping our personal identities and is fundamental to our sense of self. The ways we present ourselves—through our gender identity, cultural background, and social class—are profoundly influenced by the context and circumstances of our upbringing. Established social norms, customs, and conventions predate our existence and significantly impact the degree to which we feel free to express ourselves. Navigating our place within society can be a challenging journey, often fraught with struggles and trauma, yet it also holds the potential for positive motivation and growth.

Certain groups, such as African Americans, are profoundly affected by social pressures to conform to a majority perspective, often spending their lives suppressing their true identities to find peace and comfort. One such survival mechanism is code-switching, a practice rooted in historical and systemic racism. After the Civil War, laws enforced racial segregation and restricted the freedoms of African Americans, institutionalizing systemic racism. The author delves into the historical context of these laws, explaining their origins and implementation and the harsh consequences faced by those who resisted.

Just as my grandparents had to code-switch, so did Black Americans in what should be a more enlightened era. Despite the Civil Rights Act 1964, which aimed to transform race and gender relations, the anticipated social change has not fully materialized. Black Americans and other ethnic minorities continue to face cultural suppression and systemic discrimination, highlighting the persistence of negative social norms and conventions.

Social change has been slow, and cultural biases continue to marginalize individuals. The literature suggests that relying solely on social change to transform culture is insufficient. The psyche of individuals affected by cultural suppression perpetuates these biases across generations. Efforts to address cultural limitations such as those imposed on African Americans must include strategies to heal the soul of a people, empowering them to rise above bias. Intrinsic motivation must be foundational in forming self-identity.

Reflection Questions
Chapter Four

I. How would it feel to mask your true self to gain acceptance or obtain something that holds deep significance?

II. How does cultural background influence an individual's progression through Marcia's identity statuses, particularly in exploration and commitment?

III. In what ways can cultural expectations shape the process of identity achievement, and how might they create challenges or opportunities for self-discovery?

CHAPTER FIVE

FROZEN IN MIND: THE PSYCHOLOGY OF CULTURAL SUPPRESSION

Impact of Cultural Suppression

My dad worked sixteen-hour shifts for many years, eagerly anticipating weekends to immerse himself in football, baseball, or basketball. I dreaded those weekends because his unwavering focus on the games meant we never ventured beyond school, the grocery store, or, occasionally, the mall. Offseason, especially those without the Olympics, was a reprieve, often bringing trips to my grandparents' house. Dad would gather the family, and we would embark on the fifty-mile journey to his parents' home. Upon arrival, my brothers and I would burst into the house, greeted with wet, sloppy kisses and the aroma of Southern fried chicken, mashed potatoes, gravy, green peas, and corn pudding—my dad's favorites. We would unfold our TV trays, take seats, and relish the feast, topped off with Grandma's chocolate cake, a rare and cherished dessert.

As I started grade school, I noticed a shift in my parents' communication—it became more visceral and intense. It seemed that in a very short space of time, their relationship plummeted, leading to separation and eventually divorce. The growing hostility turned violent, culminating in a brutal altercation that remains etched in my memory. When I recount that day to my older brothers, I am struck by how we seem to remember it differently. Their recollections are faint and fragmented, as though the event did not leave the same deep imprint on them. My younger brother, being so small at the time, has no memory of it at all. However, my older brothers view the situation as more complex, suggesting that tensions between our parents may have escalated from both sides, making it difficult to blame one person alone. It is a perspective I struggle to understand fully. Intellectually, I can acknowledge the possibility of shared fault, but emotionally, it feels impossible to reconcile with what I experienced. The violence I witnessed and the helplessness I felt that day left scars that still ache. For me, the memory is vivid, raw, and deeply personal, while my brothers seem to have processed it in ways that allow them to move forward. I often wonder why we each carried such different pieces of the same moment. Did the event affect me more profoundly, or have they found ways to heal that I have not?

This contrast in how we experienced and processed the same event often makes me reflect on resilience within families and broader societal contexts. How do some people seem less encumbered by personal or systemic adversity while others bear wounds that linger for a lifetime? I think about members of marginalized groups and how they navigate bias and systemic oppression. While some individuals appear to transcend these barriers with remarkable strength, others are deeply impacted, their potential stifled by the weight of their circumstances. Observers from majority groups may acknowledge the existence of bias yet remain largely unaffected by its consequences, creating an imbalance in understanding and empathy.

This disparity reminds me of Maslow's Hierarchy of Needs. Could a similar continuum exist for how cultural and social suppression affects individuals? Perhaps some have access to support systems or internal coping mechanisms that buffer against the worst effects of adversity, while others are left vulnerable, exposed to its full force. My brothers and I experienced the same traumatic event. However, our responses were shaped by factors I do not fully understand—emotional disposition, age, memory, or perhaps even how we processed our relationship with our parents. This leaves me wondering: is resilience innate, or is it shaped by our environment, opportunities, and support networks?

Culture is like the wind: invisible yet profoundly impactful. Life is smooth when it blows in your favor, and progress comes easily. Nevertheless, when it blows against you, every step feels like an uphill battle (Walker & Soule, 2017). This adverse wind is a relentless jet stream for some, constantly pushing them back. This unyielding resistance creates a dissonance, as they are judged inadequate based on superficial traits. While this may not be true in every aspect of life, a prevailing sense of inferiority often exists when one's identity does not align with society's highest standards. When the cultural wind blows against you, its force and impact seem to depend on the resilience of your self-concept. Those with a strong foundation who are not reliant on societal acceptance can weather these pressures. However, for those who struggle with belonging and connection, cultural opposition can be suffocating.

In grade school, I was included in the gifted and talented student group, a focal point of the public school system at the time. I enjoyed this status, allowing me to participate in more exclusive programs typically found only in private schools. One such program was a performing arts initiative that began when I was in the fourth grade. Though not regularly funded, the program brought a performing arts teacher to our school about once a week, and I attended her class for an hour each session.

Despite the school predominantly serving Black children, the acting troupe, including myself, was mainly composed of a few White students. This was wonderful for me since they were already my friends. I was given a small part in a production planned for a student audience in early spring. My role included a memorable one-liner: "Hi, my name is Charles Fishbone from "A and P Weeeooo!" Moreover, I am here to interview this brave young man!" Charles Fishburn was a well-known local news anchor, and my onstage persona was instantly recognizable.

I delivered my line with flamboyant theatrical gestures, occasionally slipping into a southern drawl for added flair. The audience responded with enthusiastic applause, making me feel like a true star, even if only for a moment. These formative experiences sparked my belief that I could achieve something significant. However, I also questioned why I had not been given a more prominent role, especially given the audience's positive reaction. My friend Bill had a leading role, and I wondered why he was chosen over me.

Bill might have been the better performer, or perhaps my absence due to illness during some of the practice sessions played a role.

However, some of me suspected it because he was one of the white kids. Whether true or not, this belief led me to adopt a mindset of perceived defeat stemming from my social class. This narrative of feeling limited by my background is a common experience among those who are not part of the majority race or social group.

I constantly questioned the limits of my potential, wondering what I could achieve if not hindered by the negative perceptions of race. This curiosity evolved into exploring the effects of cultural suppression, which became the focus of my dissertation. My research concluded that cultural suppression is a systematic phenomenon perpetuated by looming sociopolitical factors, leading to pressures being mounted against a people group whose culture is suppressed.

Throughout history, conquering civilizations have subjugated those they dominated, leaving a lasting impact even after their decline. The profound effects of these conquerors, spanning various eras and regions, have significantly influenced the cultures of the subjugated peoples and shaped the course of world history.

In the late nineteenth century, beginning in the 1880s, a concerted effort emerged to strip Native Americans of their cultural identity. Clergymen, government officials, and social workers sought to assimilate Indigenous peoples into American society. Reformers, backed by the government, forcibly removed Indian children from their homes and placed them in boarding schools such as the Carlisle Indian School and the Hampton Institute. These institutions aimed to erase tribal traditions, immersing the children in American values of productivity, modesty, and sanctity.

At these schools, Indian boys and girls were acculturated and trained in vocational skills and domestic sciences, respectively. This cultural erasure extended to adults, as evangelical Protestants and Catholics endeavored to convert Native Americans, urging them to abandon their languages, clothing, and social customs in favor of a Euro-American way of life.

During this period, the federal government's policy shifted from relocating Native Americans to aggressively assimilating them into the American ideal. This involved offering land in exchange for renouncing their tribal affiliations, traditional attire, and ancestral lifestyles, thereby stripping away their cultural heritage.

American history has been constructed to largely ignore Indigenous histories and presence upon the lands now called the United States. This narrative conveniently overlooks the fact that land theft and Indigenous erasure have fundamentally shaped the country's development. We have been conditioned to accept this whitewashed, Indigenous-free account of the past as a given in American history. The Trail of Tears, one of the more widely recognized examples of dispossession, involved relocating tribes from the Southeastern United States westward toward the Mississippi River and eventually into what was known as the Indian Territory, now Oklahoma. The land stolen in this process became central to the plantation economy of the South, worked by enslaved labor to create wealth for White settler landowners (Smiles, 2021).

These relocations were just a chapter in a long history of violent dispossessions and seizures of Indigenous land in the United States. The prevailing opinion was that since Indigenous peoples were not using the land in ways settlers considered productive, the land was better off being owned and used by settlers.

What is Cultural Suppression Anyway?

When I embarked on my study investigating the origins and definition of cultural suppression, some advised me to focus on the African American experience, likely because of my identity as a Black person. This suggestion struck me as narrow-minded and even racist, as it overlooked my true motive: exploring the history of Indigenous peoples of North America. I believed this focus would offer a richer opportunity to examine cultural suppression, given that Indigenous communities perhaps have a more intact history and a deeper connection to their ancestry, allowing them to recall and articulate their lived experiences. There seemed to be more continuity among Indigenous peoples and their connection to their ancestral lands, providing a more comprehensive understanding of cultural suppression. My research intended to develop a detailed view of the cultural suppression phenomenon's meaning.

To delve deeper into this subject, the qualitative phase of my research included Indigenous North Americans who attended Indian boarding schools in the US, as they had unique experiences relevant to this topic. This research intended to hear directly from those who had been culturally suppressed to understand this concept better. Despite the lack of available research on the construct of cultural suppression, there were citations in the literature identifying Native Americans as a group that experienced cultural suppression (Verma, 2012; Gone, 2013). The inclusion of Native American participants in my study was theory-driven, where it was understood from the literature that this group was likely to have lived experiences relevant to cultural suppression as the concept being studied. This was particularly evident in how Native American children were educated in the US (Verma, 2012).

For my grounded theory study, I collected data through interviews conducted with participants by phone and in person, using a consistent set of questions. These questions were designed to elicit the participants' lived experiences and were guided by the central premise: What is cultural suppression? In grounded theory, the researcher aims to develop a general, abstract theory of a process, action, or interaction based on participants' views. This approach involves multiple stages of data collection, refining, and interrelating categories of information.

Two primary characteristics of my study's design were the constant comparison of data with emerging categories and theoretical sampling to maximize similarities and differences in the information gathered. Constant comparison ensured that new data were continually checked against existing categories to refine and expand them, while theoretical sampling allowed for a strategic selection of participants to ensure a comprehensive understanding of cultural suppression from various perspectives. This iterative process helped build a robust and nuanced theory grounded in the participants' experiences.

Indigenous American Reflections on Cultural Suppression

Identifying Indigenous American participants for my study proved to be a significant challenge as Native advocates and leaders had warned me during our informal pre-research discussions. Following the theoretical sampling approach, I contacted Indigenous American leaders who generously shared insights about their culture and way of life. These leaders provided invaluable guidance and, in some cases, helped me connect with others willing to share their experiences.

FINDING CULTURAL ACUITY

My first contact was with a group of Native Americans who had recently participated in a documentary about their experiences in Indian boarding schools. This documentary highlighted the profound cultural suppression they endured, aligning with Verma's (2012) discussion. Initially, my communication with one of the group's sponsors was promising. She responded enthusiastically and provided me with contact information for the documentary participants.

However, despite multiple attempts to reach out, I received no response. The sponsor who had initially been so helpful also ceased communication, despite my persistent follow-up calls and emails. This pattern of nonresponsiveness became a recurring theme throughout my efforts to engage the Indigenous American community.

The process was marked by a series of setbacks and moments of frustration, yet it also underscored the deep-seated mistrust and protective stance many Native Americans understandably held. Their reluctance to participate highlighted the historical wounds and ongoing impacts of cultural suppression, making my study's objectives all the more poignant and significant.

Despite setbacks in my research, I found new pathways through the wisdom and insights of Indigenous American leaders, such as Dr. Negiel Bigpond. Interviewing Dr. Bigpond was a transformative experience, providing profound perspectives for my study. He shared that engaging the Native community often proves challenging due to many historical and cultural reasons (N. Bigpond, personal communication, May 25, 2016).

Dr. Bigpond's history is a testament to these difficulties. He attended an Indian boarding school, an experience so painful that many, including himself, find it hard to recount. He vividly described the cultural suppression enforced upon the students, where they were prohibited from expressing their identity through their appearance, religion, language, or any other evident way. Corporal punishment was the harsh tool used by school officials to enforce this suppression.

One particularly heartbreaking story he shared involved a close friend who was brutally beaten for refusing to cease sharing the Native American way of life. This incident highlighted the severe measures taken to erase cultural identity. During our conversation, Dr. Bigpond also shared a powerful Native adage, passed down through oral traditions and believed to have originated during the Trail of Tears—a period of forced relocation and suffering for many Native Americans. He first recited it in his native Yuchi language: "Ha-le-e-go-no," which translates to "Always go forward, never look back" (N. Bigpond, personal communication, May 25, 2016). This phrase embodies a spirit of resilience and forward-thinking, a refusal to let past pain dictate the future.

This mindset, Dr. Bigpond explained, might partly account for the reluctance of some individuals to participate in my study. He also shared another wisdom imparted to him as a child: "Do not be like me; do better." This encouragement to surpass the achievements of one's predecessors underscores the profound cultural value of continuous improvement and resilience.

Through these narratives, I gained a deeper understanding of the complexities and emotional depths of engaging with the Native community. Dr. Bigpond's insights were academic revelations and heartfelt lessons in cultural perseverance and dignity.

Despite facing numerous setbacks, I employed various strategies to identify Native American research participants. My journey began with reaching out to Indian boarding school alumni associations, but my inquiries were met with silence. Undeterred, I extended my efforts beyond the United States, contacting several Native American tribes in other states, yet none consented to participate. Turning my focus back home, I randomly sampled from a list of thirty-nine recognized Native tribes in Oklahoma, only to find that over 90 percent did not respond to my requests.

Amid this struggle, a glimmer of hope appeared when a representative from the Quapaw Tribe of Oklahoma agreed to present my request to their Cultural Committee. After this connection, I received a list of potential candidates willing to participate in my research. However, not all listed individuals followed through with the interviews.

Ultimately, I secured seven participants for my study. Though ten interviews were initiated, three were left incomplete. The final sample represented a cross-section of twelve Oklahoma Native American tribes. Most of these participants had attended Indian boarding schools, and those who had not were raised by parents or grandparents who had. The average age of the participants was seventy-six years.

Each participant noted that they were "obviously" of Native American heritage, possessing distinct features characteristic of their ancestry. For example, the male participants mentioned keeping their hair long, a custom deeply rooted in tribal traditions. While only one participant was not originally from Oklahoma, all had spent their childhoods in the state, even if they no longer resided there.

Most participants identified themselves as leaders within the Native American community, adding depth and insight to their contributions. Their stories and experiences painted a vivid picture of resilience and cultural pride, enriching the tapestry of my research.

In constructing the survey tool, I aimed to allow Native American respondents to describe their experiences and beliefs regarding the suppression of their culture. Participants were asked to define cultural suppression and share whether they felt it was part of their experience. Remarkably, although none of the respondents had identical experiences, they all conveyed similar narratives of cultural suppression. They unanimously affirmed that their culture had been suppressed. Two participants described experiences mirroring those of others but did not consider themselves culturally suppressed. They were prohibited from communicating with family or tribal members, and their school experiences were marked by efforts to eradicate their cultural heritage. This might align with Dr. Bigpond's assertion that some individuals avoid revisiting these painful experiences due to cultural customs that discourage dwelling on the past.

Patterns emerged in the respondents' descriptions of cultural suppression, with many focusing on its impact on their people. Participants were asked to describe the emotions associated with cultural suppression. While some viewed it as a catalyst for resilience and adaptability, most associated it with negative emotions such as anger and frustration. They attributed cultural suppression to governmental actions or negative social perceptions and behaviors. Generally, they felt that cultural suppression occurs when one culture seeks to exploit another for its benefit. Respondents frequently perceived other groups as more privileged and felt that these groups held derogatory and prejudiced views toward Native Americans.

A significant theme was the suppression of religious freedom. Participants noted that their religion was uniquely targeted and suppressed in the nation, leading to a loss of traditions that may never be recovered. This suppression fostered a distrust that persisted even when practicing their religion became permissible. Many respondents reported that their people refrained from teaching cultural and religious practices to avoid discrimination, leading to feelings of inferiority.

The participants' awareness of cultural differences often began in early childhood, with elementary school being a common reference point. The repudiation of their ancestral language, whether forced or voluntary, was a strong indicator of cultural suppression. Although participants primarily discussed the collective impact on Native people, they often conveyed a sense of personal resilience in overcoming cultural suppression.

Most participants had attended Indian boarding schools, where they retained their cultural perspectives despite the suppressive environment. They described these schools as places where speaking their language openly was prohibited, highlighting the differences between Native students and others. When asked, "Are you Native American?" all respondents immediately affirmed their identity, often referencing their culture to support their claim.

The majority agreed that providing educational opportunities about Native heritage would strengthen their culture. They emphasized the importance of educating both members of their cultural group and those outside it to foster greater understanding and respect.

After analyzing the data collected from my research, four distinct categories emerged, each describing various aspects and processes of cultural suppression: Intercultural Effects of Cultural Suppression, Intracultural Effects of Cultural Suppression, Internalization of the Effects of Cultural Suppression, and Development of Cultural Acuity.

Darryl Washington, D.Ed.

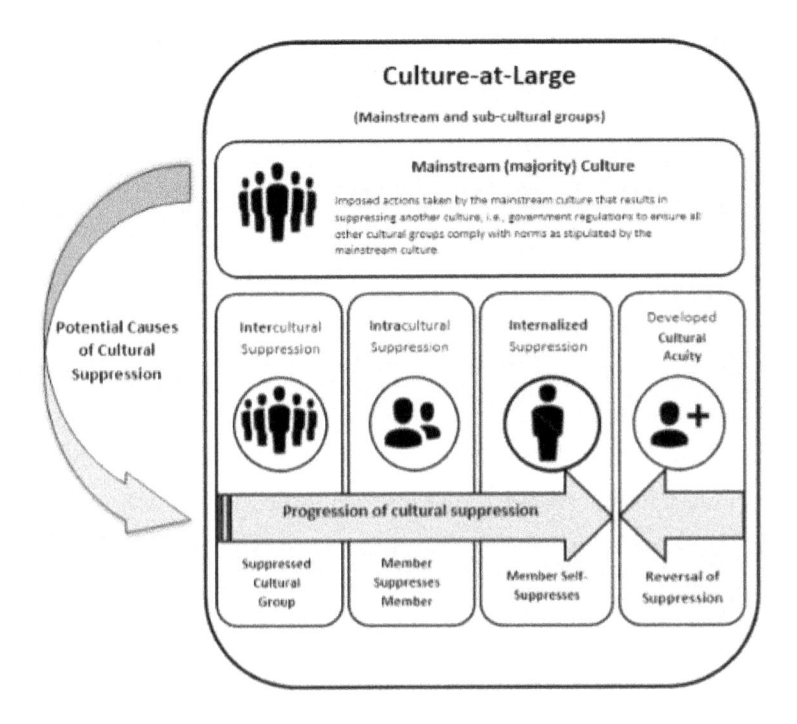

Figure 1. Summary of the theory of cultural suppression, illustrating the key components and their relationships as identified in Washington's research. From *A mixed methods study exploring the prevalence of cultural suppression among international students studying at universities in the United States* (Washington, 2017)

Intercultural Effects of Cultural Suppression (InterECS) refers to external forces that impose suppressive influences on a cultural group by a more dominant culture. This process effectively overwrites or negates the cultural identity of the suppressed group. According to the Native American participants in the study, the US government played a significant role in their cultural suppression. They highlighted historical events like the Trail of Tears and the Indian Removal Act as pivotal moments in this process. The government, motivated by greed, used laws and governance to force Native Americans to conform to mainstream American norms, resulting in the marginalization and exploitation of their culture.

Participants likened this cultural suppression to imperialism, describing it as a deliberate effort to capitalize on their wealth and resources. Institutions such as Indian boarding schools were instrumental in this process, stripping Native children of their heritage and instilling American values. The overarching theme of InterECS is the clash of cultural groups, with one culture imposing its way of life on another, leading to the marginalized status of the suppressed culture within mainstream society.

Intracultural Effects of Cultural Suppression (IntraECS) occur when members within a cultural group prevent others from acquiring essential knowledge and experiences necessary for full cultural immersion. Unlike InterECS, where one culture opposes another, IntraECS involves a culture turning against itself. This often manifests within familial relationships, where parents and grandparents discourage their children from learning and speaking their native language to help them assimilate into the dominant culture.

Participants shared how this internal suppression affected their ability to fully participate in their culture. Social ostracism within their cultural group for not conforming to traditional practices further perpetuated IntraECS. This phenomenon highlights the complex dynamics of acculturation, where adaptation is forced within the cultural group, leading to internal conflict and stress.

Internalized Effects of Cultural Suppression (IECS) describe the psychological impact of cultural suppression on individuals within the suppressed group. The negative stereotypes and disparaging treatment over decades have led to internalized poor self-perception among Native Americans. Participants shared how these negative influences infiltrated their psyche, resulting in low self-esteem and internalized conflict regarding their identity.

The development of ethnic identity is fraught with challenges in a society that suppresses one's culture. Ethnic children often internalize negative images and stereotypes from the wider society, institutions, and media. The Native American participants echoed this sentiment, indicating that the cultural suppression they experienced led to negative outcomes, both individually and collectively.

Despite the overwhelming acknowledgment of cultural suppression, many respondents demonstrated a strong sense of cultural acuity, which seemed to mitigate the effects of suppression in their lives. They had developed personal attributes that helped them overcome social impediments, such as negative stereotyping and discrimination. These individuals engaged in culturally enriching activities, such as learning their native language and participating in tribal organizations, reinforcing their cultural identity.

The development of cultural acuity appears to be a critical determinant in whether or not cultural suppression affects an individual. Respondents who were actively involved in their culture and embraced their heritage reported feeling less impacted by suppression. They unanimously agreed that education and promotion of Native culture, both within their community and beyond, were essential to counteract cultural suppression.

The research highlighted the multifaceted nature of cultural suppression among Native Americans. The intercultural and intracultural effects, along with the internalization of negative influences, paint a complex picture of the challenges faced by Native communities. However, the development of cultural acuity provides a hopeful narrative of resilience and strength. Participants emphasized the importance of education and cultural promotion as key strategies to mitigate the effects of cultural suppression and foster a more inclusive and respectful society.

The awareness of cultural suppression often begins in the earliest stages of development, casting a long shadow over many individuals' lives and influencing every aspect of their existence. Numerous testimonials reveal a striking consistency: Many people first encountered cultural suppression in elementary school, while others perceived it earlier within their families. These early recognitions of suppression were primarily attributed to external forces, particularly government influence.

Individuals described how a dominant culture imposes its will on a less dominant one, creating an environment where members of the suppressed culture are compelled to enforce these external demands on each other. Participants frequently noted that their culture was perceived as less affluent compared to mainstream American culture. This perception often led to internalized feelings of inferiority, affecting their self-image and how the broader society viewed them.

Many participants strongly believed that failing to assimilate into the mainstream culture would result in negative consequences. Their lived experiences generally supported this belief, reinforcing the notion that noncompliance with the dominant culture's norms and values would lead to adverse outcomes.

Cultural suppression is a systematic phenomenon driven by overarching sociopolitical factors, such as governance and laws imposed by the suppressing culture. These factors pressure the suppressed culture significantly, compelling its members to assimilate to avoid potential repercussions. This suppression is further sustained by societal standards set and enforced by the dominant culture.

Familial relationships within suppressed cultures often contribute to this phenomenon, as some families may discourage or forbid their members from learning their native language or traditional means of communication. This internal enforcement perpetuates the cycle of suppression, embedding it deeply within the fabric of the affected culture.

Development of Cultural Acuity

Analyzing the data, it became clear that while respondents acknowledged cultural suppression, many distinctly negated its impact on their lives. Despite recalling early life stages where expressing their culture was prohibited, they largely did not perceive themselves as culturally suppressed. Instead, they emphasized personal attributes developed to overcome social impediments like negative stereotyping and discrimination.

Initially, their success appeared due to assimilating into mainstream American culture. However, further analysis revealed that those who reported being unaffected by cultural suppression had developed a profound understanding and embrace of their innate culture. This development of cultural acuity (DCA) emerged as a key factor in mitigating the effects of cultural suppression.

The respondents actively engaged in culturally enriching activities, such as learning their native language or participating in organizations supporting Native American causes. They spoke proudly, demonstrating a deep awareness of their history and traditions. When discussing the broader challenges faced by their people, they indicated that those most affected by cultural suppression were often unaware of their cultural heritage.

Unanimously, they agreed that addressing cultural suppression would require education and the promotion of Native culture, both within their communities and beyond. Through these efforts, they believed cultural suppression could be effectively countered, fostering a stronger and more resilient cultural identity.

Finding cultural acuity is the transformative moment when an individual who has endured cultural suppression gains profound clarity and acceptance of their own cultural beliefs, social customs, racial traits, religion or traditions, and the shared attitudes, values, goals, and practices that define their social identity. This cognitive and emotional harmony empowers the individual to transcend the dominant cultural perspectives and dictates. Achieving cultural acuity enables a person to live a meaningful and fulfilling life free from the mental strongholds and societal expectations that once constrained them.

Darryl Washington, D.Ed.

Reflection Questions

Chapter Five

I. What does cultural acuity mean for you?

_____

II. How might you influence the end of cultural suppression?

_____

III. Were any of your ancestors culturally suppressed?

_____

CHAPTER SIX

FINDING CULTURAL ACUITY

Cultural Intelligence: The Engine That Can

My maternal grandfather passed away from cancer when I was about three years old. While our relationship had not yet flourished, his legacy influenced my desire for lifelong learning. He was remarkably intelligent, a science teacher by profession and a chemist by training—a true Renaissance man. His basement workshop was a hive of activity filled with diverse projects and research, reflecting his boundless curiosity and intellect. I often wonder about the impact he may have made in ensuring the success of his children and grandchildren had he lived longer. As the only university graduate in our family holding a master's degree, he stood as a beacon of academic achievement.

It was not until I was older after he had passed away, that I learned about my grandfather's affinity for assessing his children and grandchildren to gauge our intelligence. He had a predilection for those he deemed more intelligent. Grandad was an only child, and I wonder to what extent this may have been an internal need of his to project an inner duality onto his children, seeing us as an extension of his idealized self and his repressed shadow self.

But I vividly remember being under his scrutiny, having my turn at being examined. When I was about two, my mom placed me in his bedroom to play under his supervision while she and my grandmother attended to something important. Though I was supposed to be under his care, I felt his intense gaze upon me as I played with a toy, even though he did not speak.

I likely could not carry on a conversation at that age, but I have clear memories and emotions tied to this encounter. Our eyes locked in a silent contest until I finally looked away, conceding defeat. He roused himself from a reclining position and swung his legs around me, framing me on both sides. I recall his large, white feet flanking my toddler-sized body. I examined his right foot intensely, thinking, "What big feet does Grandad have? They are so much whiter than mine. Why are we so different?"

Curious, he asked, "What do you see? What are you looking at?" His scientist's mind seemed intrigued by my curiosity. He seemed to understand that I was comparing our differences, trying to grasp our contrast. Oddly, at that moment, I felt I had somehow impressed him; his pleasure with my investigation was evident. He encouraged me to continue exploring, showing a genuine interest in my inquisitiveness. For the first time in my young life, whether he was intentional or not, the event was somehow affirming, and it secured a sense of belonging. Granddad's apparent pride in me brought me clarity and self-acceptance. It was an epiphany where I saw myself as having some value.

Those affected by cultural suppression often find themselves forced to conform to the standards of the majority, which undermines the development of a positive self-identity. This relentless pressure leads to constant negative self-talk as individuals compare themselves to an often-unattainable norm, fostering a sense of self-loathing for their perceived imperfections. I distinctly remember thinking how much better my granddad's foot looked than mine because it was much lighter in tone. However, I also recall his special attention and how it positively affected my inner dialogue. Instead of comparing our differences, I focused on the kinship we shared. This shift in perspective changed how I was thinking about myself. When we can find connections with others who are like us in some way—whether through family, ethnicity, or religion—we lay the foundation for belonging, connection, and self-affirmation.

Freedom from cultural suppression is developing cultural acuity (DCA), a transformative journey where one's focus shifts from mainstream values and norms to a richer, more expansive understanding of oneself in culture. It is a journey that allows individuals to appreciate the broader spectrum of human experience. Many who have embarked on this path expressed a deep, lifelong desire to become more connected with their cultural heritage. They yearned to immerse themselves in their ancestors' traditions, stories, and customs, seeking a sense of identity and belonging that transcends the surface level of societal norms. Conversely, some shared regret, reflecting on the missed opportunities to engage with their community. They spoke of a sense of loss, having been denied the chance to participate in the vibrant tapestry of their cultural heritage, longing for a deeper connection with their people.

In my research on the development of cultural acuity, I found that true liberation from cultural suppression is achieved through self-discovery that begins by exploring one's generational and cultural heritage. Cultural acuity—the self-awareness, clarity, and acceptance of both one's own culture and others—emerged as a powerful tool in this process. A key insight was that individuals who developed cultural acuity not only gained a deeper understanding of their own cultural identity but often became advocates for the well-being of other cultures, especially those who had experienced similar forms of cultural suppression.

This connection between cultural acuity and cultural intelligence (CQ) is significant. While my research did not rely on the CQ model, I discovered that individuals who developed CQ often sought cultural acuity. As their cultural intelligence grew—enhancing their capacity to understand and engage with diverse cultures—they were driven to achieve a deeper, more personal relationship with culture. This led them to seek greater self-awareness and acceptance, not only of their own cultural identity but also of the broader human experience.

The individuals in my research who developed cultural acuity showed a remarkable capacity for empathy and respect and a deep appreciation for cultural diversity. While my research did not rely on the CQ model, I observed that those who attained CQ naturally progressed toward cultural acuity. As they expanded their understanding and engagement with other cultures, they sought to deepen their self-awareness and acceptance of both their own cultural roots and those of others. This pursuit of cultural acuity became a path to greater cultural enlightenment, fostering a holistic appreciation for the richness and interconnectedness of the human experience.

Developing cultural intelligence involves the ability to adapt and navigate challenges that arise in interactions with people or artifacts from cultures different from one's own. Unlike general intelligence, cultural intelligence is more nuanced, and not everyone has a natural inclination toward understanding or discerning it. Cultural intelligence encompasses a practical, tacit-knowledge-based component, making it like what is sometimes referred to as practical intelligence, which is somewhat distinct from general intelligence, which is based on one's ability to apply their knowledge in the real world (Hedlund, 2020; Sternberg & Hedlund, 2002). Cultural intelligence can be broken down into metacognitive, cognitive, motivational, and behavioral components (Ang et al. 2006, 2007, 2015). A combination of typical and maximum performance measures is advisable to fully measure cultural intelligence. Research indicates that these two measures evaluate different aspects of cultural intelligence (Sternberg et al., 2021).

Cultural intelligence is a complex and layered construct. Robert Sternberg conceptualized "intelligence" as the ability to operate proficiently in a specific context, identifying four essential components: motivation, cognition, metacognition, and behavioral adaptability. Cultural intelligence builds upon these principles, presenting four distinct dimensions rooted in Sternberg's comprehensive theoretical framework of diverse loci of intelligence. Distinct from many other models of intercultural competence, CQ is firmly grounded in theory. Each dimension of cultural intelligence encapsulates a unique facet of the broader capability to navigate and perform successfully in multicultural environments. These four dimensions collectively form the foundation of cultural intelligence, each contributing critically to an individual's overall cultural effectiveness. Earley and Ang built on Sternberg and Detterman's multiple loci framework on intelligence to argue that intelligence must go beyond mere cognitive abilities. Ang and Van Dyne developed an initial nomological network of predictors and outcomes of the four key CQ capabilities:

- **CQ Drive (Motivational CQ):** The level of a person's interest, persistence, and confidence to function in culturally diverse settings
- **CQ Knowledge (Cognitive CQ):** The level of a person's understanding of how cultures are similar and how they are different
- **CQ Strategy (Metacognitive CQ):** The degree to which a person plans for, remains aware during, and checks after multicultural interactions
- **CQ Action (Behavioral CQ):** The extent of a person's flexibility and appropriate use of a broad repertoire of behaviors and skills during multicultural encounters

Cultural intelligence has become increasingly important in today's interconnected and interdependent world. As globalization accelerates and intercultural interactions become ubiquitous, the need to understand and respect different cultural norms is more critical than ever. Historically, cultural intelligence was considered a luxury—a skill reserved for diplomats, travelers, or those interested in anthropology. In the past, many people could live their entire lives within the familiar confines of their own communities, seldom encountering individuals from vastly different cultures (Sternberg et al., 2022). However, in our modern era of rapid globalization, such insular experiences are increasingly rare. Interactions between people from diverse cultural backgrounds have multiplied, bringing with them the potential for both enrichment and conflict.

One key source of misunderstanding is the significant variation in cultural norms, including those governing gender interactions. For instance, what is deemed appropriate in male-female dynamics in one society might be considered highly unconventional or offensive in another, as highlighted by Wood and Eagly (2002). These disparities in values and behaviors can lead to friction when one culture imposes its expectations on another without understanding the underlying context. Such cultural clashes emphasize the necessity of developing cultural intelligence—a skill that goes beyond knowledge to encompass the ability to interpret, adapt, and thrive in multicultural settings.

In this evolving global landscape, cultural intelligence is no longer optional; it is an essential tool for navigating the complexities of human diversity. It provides a framework for understanding how individuals from different cultures think, feel, and act—perspectives that may initially seem baffling to outsiders. Importantly, this understanding is not just about improving our relationships with those from other cultures but also about deepening our awareness of our own cultural identities. Through intercultural interactions, we can see our own norms, traditions, and assumptions as one approach among many rather than the universal standard.

Cultural intelligence invites us to step into a broader worldview where differences are not tolerated but actively explored and appreciated. It challenges us to move beyond simplistic categorizations of "right" or "wrong" ways of thinking and behaving, encouraging a more nuanced appreciation of human diversity. As our lives become increasingly intertwined with those of people from other cultures, the ability to navigate these differences with empathy and insight will be a defining skill of the 21st century.

Cross-cultural collaboration has emerged as a vital element in today's interconnected world, demanding the focused attention of educators (Senad Bećirović, 2023). In our increasingly global society, students frequently engage with individuals from diverse cultural backgrounds in person and through digital platforms. This dynamic is particularly pronounced in regions like the Balkan peninsula, where, especially in Bosnia and Herzegovina, the rich tapestry of cultural diversity has historically been intertwined with ethnic conflict, particularly during the turbulent 1990s.

In such contexts, there is an urgent necessity to cultivate and refine cultural intelligence and intercultural competencies. These critical skills enable students from varied backgrounds to work together harmoniously and effectively. The goal is to foster academic and cultural growth and facilitate progress across economic and social spheres.

In essence, societies grappling with diverse cultural landscapes face significant challenges: achieving effective task performance, overcoming cultural barriers, and fostering meaningful cooperation among members of multicultural teams. Addressing these issues is crucial for harnessing the full potential of cross-cultural interactions and driving collective success. For instance, men raised in cultures that traditionally show a lack of respect for women might not have previously considered alternative perspectives. Exposure to different cultures can reveal that the way women are treated in their society is not an unchangeable truth but rather a choice that may be less than ideal (Sternberg et al. 2022). This awareness can be transformative, leading to a reevaluation of long-held beliefs and behaviors.

Moreover, the ability to navigate and understand diverse cultures—cultural intelligence—is a skill that can be developed, provided there is a genuine motivation to do so. While some aspects of cultural intelligence may seem like common sense, it is more accurately described as a form of tacit knowledge gained through experience (Sternberg and Hedlund 2002). Although rooted in lived experiences, cultural intelligence can also be cultivated through deliberate learning.

People can enhance their ability to engage effectively with individuals from diverse cultural backgrounds by reflecting on their experiences and receiving targeted instruction.

Culturally, Intelligently Driven

Growing up, my understanding of the world and its diverse peoples was limited. My perceptions were shaped by what I read in books or saw on television. Current events reached me through news broadcasts or the daily newspaper, which often painted a grim picture of the world beyond our borders. Nations that made headlines usually did so due to wars, natural disasters, or other alarming events. This constant stream of troubling news made traveling abroad seem daunting, and I found little desire to venture beyond the safety of my home in the United States. Raised with a nationalist perspective, I believed there was no place like home, and the world outside seemed both unfamiliar and intimidating.

Although initially hesitant about venturing into foreign lands, something undeniably magnetic about the sounds of different dialects and languages captivated my soul. I discovered that I had a natural talent for imitating accents from various parts of the world, and this playful skill brought me great joy. My curiosity, which is generally strong, is particularly piqued by relationships and people—especially those who bring a sense of diversity into my world. I have a deep, genuine desire to understand their perspectives and grasp what holds significance in their lives.

In fourth grade, I befriended Simon, an Australian classmate. I loved listening to him speak and eagerly asked him endless questions about his life in Australia. His distinct accent and willingness to share his experiences ignited my curiosity about the world beyond my immediate surroundings. While I was cautious about engaging with other cultures, I was always eager to learn about them. Looking back, it is clear that my cultural intelligence was beginning to take root.

CQ drive, also known as motivational cultural intelligence, reflects a person's interest, persistence, and confidence in navigating culturally diverse settings. Deep curiosity and a desire for novel experiences often spark this drive. Each time I encountered someone from another country—whether in a store or on the street—I was filled with awe and an insatiable curiosity. I would silently observe, wondering what life might be like in their homelands, imagining the vibrant colors, sounds, and rhythms that defined their daily lives. More than anything, I was captivated by what set them apart from people like me or those I was more familiar with. The pursuit of understanding their culture and its unique qualities became a source of fascination for me, a bridge that connected us and celebrated the rich tapestry of human experience.

Curiosity plays a crucial role in our ability to successfully navigate a multicultural social environment, where understanding those around us is essential (Foster 2004). It shapes how we communicate, relate, and stay connected to one another, serving as the foundation for developing CQ drive and enhancing our cultural learning. By embracing curiosity, we seek knowledge of the social world, satisfying a need for effective control over our environment (Kashdan et al., 2020). Imagine stepping into a new country for the first time, eager to explore and make the most of your experience. To truly immerse yourself, you must be willing to ask questions and engage with the locals, enriching your journey. Interpersonally curious people tend to be more socially competent, sociable, and capable of building networks of relationships that offer support during life's challenges.

Feelings Drive CQ

For those with an unquenchable thirst for exploration, the journey is driven by more than a simple desire to see new places. It is fueled by a profound yearning to immerse themselves in the tapestry of the world's cultures, expand their understanding beyond the superficial, and truly appreciate the depth and diversity of human experience. These travelers are not content with merely learning facts about different regions or people; they seek a deeper connection that allows them to integrate seamlessly into any cultural setting. Their journey is transformative, enabling them to forge meaningful and authentic bonds with individuals from all walks of life, regardless of the backdrop against which they meet.

CQ drive measures your emotional response to intercultural scenarios, reflecting how you feel when navigating interactions across different cultures. It assesses your willingness and motivation to engage with and adapt to unfamiliar cultural environments. High CQ drive indicates a strong ability to persevere through the stress and disorientation often accompanying intercultural experiences.

In the article "University Student Responses to Intercultural Scenarios: Contact Strategies and Perceptions of Otherness" by Ana Sofia Hofmeyr, the focus is on how first-year university students at international institutions handle intercultural interactions. The study delves into these students' strategies and perceptions when encountering people from different cultural backgrounds. The findings reveal that students generally approach these interactions with openness and respect, particularly in formal settings where clear guidelines are present. However, they face greater challenges in informal situations, especially when physical contact is involved. Despite their initial openness, students still tend to view those from other cultures as outsiders, unfamiliar with their language and cultural norms. This research highlights the context-dependent nature of intercultural competence (IC). It suggests that although students are willing to engage in intercultural interactions, deep-seated perceptions of otherness can influence their experiences. The study's insights are crucial for universities aiming to enhance their students' intercultural competence, preparing them to thrive in an increasingly interconnected world.

CQ drive invokes a desire in individuals to explore and connect, which is rooted in intrinsic motivation. This powerful internal force compels individuals to engage in activities for the sheer joy and fulfillment they bring. Intrinsic motivation is like a guiding flame, igniting actions fueled by personal interest, curiosity, and a genuine desire to master a skill or achieve a goal. It is not about seeking external rewards or recognition; it is about the satisfaction of doing something purely for the love of it. This type of motivation thrives on the pleasure derived from the activity, making it a powerful force that sustains enthusiasm and commitment over time.

Intrinsic motivation can manifest in several ways. First, there is the natural interest or enjoyment in a task. When a person finds a particular task fascinating or delightful, they are driven to engage fully, often exceeding expectations—for example, a researcher who is captivated by their field of study and relishes the creative process. For these individuals, the work itself becomes its reward.

The pursuit of mastery represents another facet of intrinsic motivation. Those motivated to enhance their skills and competence are drawn to challenges that foster growth. This is evident in the employee who eagerly takes on a difficult project, not just for the immediate outcomes but as an opportunity to refine their abilities. The satisfaction gained from skill development fuels a continuous cycle of self-improvement and determination.

Intrinsic motivation thrives in environments where individuals feel a strong sense of autonomy and control over their work. When employees are entrusted with the freedom to make decisions, exercise their creativity, and influence their work environment, their intrinsic motivation reaches new heights. University professors, who are as deeply immersed in theoretical exploration as they are in imparting knowledge to students, exemplify this dynamic. In such scenarios, intrinsic motivation is significantly amplified by the empowerment that accompanies guiding one's professional journey, fostering a deep sense of purpose and fulfillment.

Understanding these various forms of intrinsic motivation allows organizations to cultivate strategies that tap into these deep drive sources. By acknowledging and nurturing these aspects of employee motivation, workplaces can create environments that meet employees' fundamental psychological needs and foster a lasting passion for their work.

On the other hand, individuals indifferent to the cultural fabric that defines a society may find it challenging to adapt to its subtleties. However, a remarkable transformation occurs when one is committed to truly understanding and immersing oneself in a new cultural environment. The mind expands, embracing a world of possibilities that were previously unimaginable. Cultural differences, once viewed as obstacles or inconveniences, become sources of fascination and excitement. The effort to learn about another culture ignites curiosity and wonder, turning the complexities of cultural diversity into a deeply enriching experience.

Adopting another's cultural perspective can be complicated, because it can be difficult to truly understand the thoughts and decisions of individuals from different cultural backgrounds. Although cultural competency can help reduce misunderstandings during intercultural encounters, those who are culturally inexperienced can misinterpret the intentions and beliefs of a culture, not their own, attributing thoughts based on their cultural context rather than that of the people group they may encounter. There is a real challenge when some attempt to adopt a cross-cultural perspective, and instead of haphazardly entering cross-cultural engagement not knowing another's perspective, one must be willing to adjust their perspective based on additional knowledge about the other person's cultural background (Rasmussen & Sieck, n.d.).

Possessing CQ drive means harboring deep motivation and sustained interest in navigating and thriving within culturally diverse settings. This quality encompasses a genuine curiosity and eagerness to engage with different cultures and the confidence to overcome the challenges these environments may present. Curiosity is a fundamental human motivation that influences learning, the acquisition of knowledge, and life fulfillment. Curiosity is about seeking information and experiences for their own sake through self-directed behavior. General overt social curiosity is an interest in other people's behaviors, thoughts, and feelings. It is an underlying motivation to understand what makes people tick rather than a tendency to initiate conversations or socialize with others. Curiosity has been described as a central human motivation, a universal human strength, and a pillar leading to human achievement. An individual with a high level of CQ drive is better equipped to adapt to new work environments, social settings, and life circumstances, even when they differ vastly from their cultural background.

CQ Drive in Motion

In culturally diverse experiences, intrinsic and extrinsic motivations intertwine, each contributing uniquely to an individual's drive and engagement. Intrinsic motivation offers intangible rewards, such as a profound sense of personal satisfaction and joy, which often deepen one's commitment to engaging with diverse cultures. Conversely, extrinsic motivation involves tangible benefits, aligning with concrete goals such as career advancement or achieving specific objectives. These motivations create a powerful impetus for individuals to immerse themselves in and thrive within culturally rich environments. In the academic sphere, those with a heightened motivational cultural intelligence (CQ) are particularly drawn to international teaching opportunities. These individuals deeply value the enriching experiences of navigating diverse cultural landscapes and are confident in their ability to handle the challenges that inevitably arise. Their enthusiasm is fueled by both the personal fulfillment they derive and the tangible rewards these global engagements can offer, driving their commitment to embrace and excel in such international roles.

However, this drive is not without its limits. In environments where cultural differences are particularly vast—referred to as high cultural distance—the effectiveness of CQ drive can be diminished, especially when adapting to work-related tasks. This nuanced understanding of

CQ drive's impact is highlighted in the study by Song et al. (2021), which delves into the relationship between motivational cultural intelligence (CQ) and the cultural adjustment of Chinese expatriates.

The study, based on data from 242 Chinese expatriates working across twenty-five countries, reveals that individuals with higher motivational CQ experience significant positive effects on their ability to adjust across three key dimensions: work adjustment, general adjustment, and interaction adjustment. In other words, these expatriates are better equipped to navigate their professional roles, acclimate to the general culture of their host country, and interact effectively with local colleagues and communities.

However, the study also finds that the extent of cultural distance can negatively influence this relationship, particularly in work adjustment. When the cultural gap between the expatriate's home country and the host country is larger, the positive impact of motivational CQ on work-related adaptation is less pronounced. This suggests that while CQ drive is a powerful tool for overcoming cultural challenges, its effectiveness may be hindered when cultural differences are too substantial.

As an example of how CQ drive is applied in real-world scenarios, in the realm of higher education, CQ drive plays a pivotal role in navigating the complexities of cultural distance. This concept, which refers to the differences in cultural contexts we encounter, is far more than a personal hurdle to overcome. It is a powerful factor shaping how we approach creativity and problem-solving. When CQ's drive is strong, it compels individuals and teams to acknowledge and embrace these cultural differences, turning them into opportunities for innovation. Research has shown that environments rich in contextual diversity—where cultural contexts vary widely—tend to foster more innovative solutions, enhance decision-making, and improve overall performance. This is because the diverse perspectives brought about by different cultural backgrounds challenge conventional thinking, pushing us to explore new ideas and approaches.

However, the challenge of cultivating such diversity, especially within academic institutions, is deeply rooted in the historical traditions of these establishments ("Context Diversity: Reframing Higher Education in the 21st Century," 2009). For instance, the US higher education system has long been entrenched in a German research model imported from Europe and superimposed on a British colonial college system. With its Eurocentric focus, this prevailing educational framework has created a learning environment that often excludes other cultural perspectives. The result is a hidden dimension of cultural context that has been largely invisible and ignored until recent times. The predominance of this academic culture not only marginalizes alternative learning environments but also perpetuates a narrow, one-dimensional approach to education.

In this context, CQ drive becomes essential for leaders and educators who seek to break free from these outdated models. By harnessing the motivational power of CQ drive, they can transform organizational cultures, making them more inclusive and better suited to the needs of diverse populations. This shift is especially critical for attracting and retaining students drawn to applied or community-oriented education. While the need for change in educational systems has long been recognized, what has been lacking is a clear model for how to achieve it.

This is where contextual diversity comes into play as a transformative paradigm. Rather than simply reforming existing structures, contextual diversity calls for a complete reframing of academic cultures to serve all populations better, particularly those historically underrepresented. CQ drive is the catalyst for this change, motivating individuals to explore, embrace, and integrate diverse cultural perspectives into the fabric of their institutions.

The challenges we face in higher education—underperformance, conflicts over cultural context, and the underrepresentation of certain groups—are not simply issues of access or critical mass. They are symptoms of a deeper problem: the need to transform the cultural context in which education occurs. By leveraging the CQ drive, educators can take charge of creating systemic change, fostering environments where diverse perspectives are welcomed and actively cultivated to fuel innovation and excellence.

Through strategies such as reframing pedagogy and curriculum—expanding and shifting educational practices without compromising quality—and rethinking the concept of diversity, institutions can begin to align with the needs and aspirations of all students. In doing so, they can create a truly inclusive learning community where the CQ drive motivates every member to engage with and learn from the richness of diverse cultural experiences.

This chapter delves into the concept of CQ drive and how it can develop in someone who initially has a limited understanding of the world's diverse cultures. Even when knowledge of other people and cultures is minimal, it does not have to limit their ability to engage effectively in cross-cultural environments. Curiosity about different ways of life can begin to take root, ignited by encounters with individuals from varied backgrounds.

The fascination with life beyond one's immediate surroundings and growing curiosity can be the seed from which CQ drive blossoms. This drive reflects a person's genuine interest, persistence, and confidence in navigating culturally diverse settings. Fueled by a deep-seated desire to understand and connect with others across cultural boundaries, CQ's drive transforms initial hesitations into a profound appreciation for human diversity. Curiosity plays a crucial role in this process, acting as a catalyst for developing CQ drive. It empowers individuals to thrive in multicultural environments by actively seeking to understand and relate to others. Cultural gaps are bridged through this curiosity, leading to a richer, more interconnected human experience.

Darryl Washington, D.Ed.

Reflection Questions
Chapter Six

I. What are the key components of cultural intelligence, and how do they interact to enhance an individual's ability to navigate diverse cultural environments?

_____

II. In what ways can developing cultural intelligence contribute to reducing bias and prejudice in personal interactions?

_____

III. What strategies can be implemented to improve your cultural intelligence over time?

_____

CHAPTER SEVEN

WHAT IS IT THAT YOU DO NOT UNDERSTAND?

Culturally Knowledgeable

Visiting my parents' families seemed like a journey into another world, a rare and cherished adventure beyond the familiar walls of our home. In those days, the concept of a "date night" was foreign, and my parents rarely stepped out together, content with the rhythms of home life. On the few occasions when they did embark on a trip out of town—so rare that I could count them on one hand—I was left in the care of my maternal grandmother while my two older brothers stayed with our paternal grandparents. My younger brother, still an infant, would accompany our parents as I had when I was the youngest. I never fully understood the reasoning behind this arrangement, though it may have seemed unusual to others to trust four boys to behave themselves without much trouble. However, I never questioned it; instead, I reveled in the special attention I received during my stay with my grandmother.

My grandmother had some of her children later in life, so my aunt and uncles, still in their teenage years, were often at home when I visited. They were not much older than I was, so my presence as a toddler did not garner much attention. What I treasured most during those visits was the luxury of sleeping in my grandmother's grand king-size bed, enveloped by the comfort of her spacious two-story home—a stark contrast to the cozy bungalow where my family lived. Her house felt like a palace, and her cooking was equally majestic, much like my dad's mother, who also had a talent for serving up generous portions that left you warm and full.

As I grew older, my visits to my dad's parents became more frequent. I loved both sets of grandparents deeply and relished the time spent with them, though each experience was distinctly different. The differences were not just between the grandparents themselves but between the entire families they represented. Each side was like a separate world with customs and traditions that shaped my upbringing in contrasting ways.

My mother's family was reserved, and their interactions were measured and formal. They were not particularly affectionate; greetings often lacked hugs and kisses, and I cannot recall much physical contact with anyone from that side. Visits were premeditated; you always called ahead and never showed up unannounced. Time together was infrequent, and the adage "Children should be seen and not heard" was more of a rule than a suggestion. My brothers and I were acknowledged rather than engaged, present but rarely the center of attention.

In stark contrast, my father's family embraced the physicality of affection, challenging the touch-me-not persona I had unconsciously adopted. Hugs, kisses, and long embraces were the norm, and family extended beyond blood relations to include the entire church community. Every visit was met with open arms, and if a meal wasn't ready when you arrived, it soon would be. Their generosity knew no bounds, and despite modest means, they shared what they had freely. My dad's family lived close to one another, forming a village where everyone was connected, and every home was open to visitors.

Spending time with my parents' families was like journeying between two distinct worlds, each with its atmosphere and expectations. My father's family embraced me with a palpable warmth, their love flowing freely and without reservation. They created a space where I felt a profound sense of belonging and could breathe easily, confident in the knowledge that I was valued just as I was. Every interaction was infused with a sense of inclusivity, their generosity extending far beyond material things—it was a generosity of spirit, an unspoken promise that I was always welcome, always cherished.

In stark contrast, my mother's family operated with a quiet, measured restraint. Their affection, though present, seemed conditional, often leaving me to weigh my actions and words, constantly assessing whether I measured up to their expectations. It was a world where love felt like it came with strings attached, where every interaction carried the subtle undertone of judgment. This environment required a different kind of navigation, one where I had to be more cautious and more aware of my place within the family dynamic.

These contrasting experiences profoundly shaped my understanding of family, love, and the essence of belonging. My father's family taught me that love could be unconditional, a gift freely given without needing approval. On the other hand, my mother's family showed me a more complex side of love, one intertwined with expectation and the need to prove oneself. Despite the differences, I learned to move between these two worlds easily, adapting to their unique ways of being and finding a sense of belonging in both.

In much the same way, understanding cultural intelligence (CQ) requires navigating the complexities of different cultural landscapes. CQ knowledge, the cognitive aspect of cultural intelligence, encompasses a deep understanding of cultural differences, the factors that shape these differences, and the ability to apply this knowledge effectively in multicultural interactions. Without a solid grasp of how cultures are similar and different, one cannot fully develop the capacity for CQ knowledge. It is about recognizing how culture influences behavior and discerning when cultural norms versus personal traits shape actions.

Knowing versus Feeling Culture

CQ knowledge involves understanding how cultures diverge in values, practices, communication styles, and other key dimensions. It is one of the four pillars of cultural intelligence (CQ), which measures an individual's ability to function effectively across various cultural contexts. As discussed in the previous chapter, CQ drive reflects your emotional response to intercultural situations; it is about your willingness and motivation to engage with and adapt to unfamiliar cultural environments.

Having CQ knowledge without CQ drive is like possessing knowledge without wisdom. It is intellectually limiting because you cannot achieve true cultural intelligence without the intrinsic motivation to apply what you know. CQ knowledge might give you the intellectual framework, but without CQ drive, that knowledge remains inert,

FINDING CULTURAL ACUITY

unable to inspire meaningful intercultural connections. In essence, understanding cultural differences is crucial, but it is the drive to engage with those differences that transform knowledge into action and wisdom.

CQ knowledge is foundational to developing cultural intelligence, encompassing a deep and multifaceted understanding of the diverse cultural backgrounds we navigate. It begins with cultural awareness—an insight into how our cultural background shapes our perceptions, behaviors, and communication. This self-awareness is critical, as it helps us recognize that what we consider normal is often a product of our specific cultural upbringing, not a universal standard—for example, I am navigating between my parents' families.

Moving beyond self-awareness, cross-cultural understanding involves grasping how other cultures operate—their norms, values, and practices, shaped by unique historical contexts and religious beliefs. This understanding extends to business and legal systems, where awareness of different regulatory environments, negotiation styles, and decision-making processes becomes crucial, especially in multicultural business settings.

Both verbal and nonverbal language play a key role in cultural exchanges. Linguistic understanding goes beyond just knowing the language; it is about appreciating the subtleties of nonverbal cues like gestures and body language, which can vary significantly across cultures.

At the heart of CQ knowledge is an appreciation of cultural norms and values. This includes understanding fundamental cultural dimensions such as individualism vs. collectivism and power distance, which influence how people interact and make decisions. The ability to balance global and local perspectives is also essential, as well as knowing how global trends intersect with local traditions and how to navigate these complexities with cultural sensitivity.

Finally, CQ knowledge emphasizes cultural learning and adaptation. It is not just about acquiring static knowledge; it is about being open to learning from each new cultural encounter, understanding that cultures evolve, and so must our understanding of them. This adaptability extends to recognizing differences in social systems and practices, which shape how education, health care, and governance function in various cultures and how these differences influence our interactions.

CQ knowledge brings together the many threads of cultural understanding, allowing us to move through different worlds confidently and respectfully. The intellectual foundation complements the emotional drive we experience in intercultural interactions, anchoring our curiosity and motivation in a deep, continuously growing understanding of the people and cultures we encounter.

Devoid of CQ

During an outing with a new acquaintance—someone who happened to be Caucasian and would eventually become significant in my life—we found ourselves immersed in a curious exchange of questions and answers, each of us eager to uncover more about the other. As we delved deeper into the conversation, the questions I was being asked began to center around race and ethnicity. At first, I was taken aback, finding the inquiries both surprising and unsettling. It felt like I was being studied like an entirely different species rather than someone with a different skin tone.

FINDING CULTURAL ACUITY

Amid our lively conversation, one question suddenly hung in the air like an unexpected chill: "What color is your God?" The words were not uttered with malice, yet they struck me profoundly, leaving a lingering sense of disheartenment. I could see in their eyes a genuine innocence, a sincere curiosity that lacked any intent to offend, but the question itself unveiled a deep chasm in understanding between us. Until that moment, I had always perceived race as merely a beautiful variation in skin tones of diversity that added richness to humanity. Being young and relatively sheltered, I had never delved into such profound discussions about race, especially not with someone older, whom I had regarded as wiser and more experienced. Though posed with pure intent, their question resonated with a startling ignorance, revealing a naivete I had not anticipated.

In hindsight, while I might have preferred a different kind of exchange during our first meeting, I now see that this was a pivotal opportunity for them to develop their cultural intelligence—both in motivation and understanding. They were learning about me as an individual of a different background, gaining valuable insights, and forging a meaningful relationship. Their growing care for me became the catalyst that motivated them to learn and embrace a broader perspective.

I did not interpret my new acquaintance's questions and remarks as prejudiced because there was no underlying hostility or preference based on race. Instead, they were trying to learn more about me. True prejudice, however, carries an intentionality rooted in contempt and a rigid judgment of others. Prejudice is not just an attitude; it is a process that can develop over time and is deeply embedded in a person's psychosocial makeup.

Darryl Washington, D.Ed.

Prejudice is a form of ignorance, and it plays a critical role in maintaining systems of racial domination, emphasizing how societal structures facilitate and perpetuate this ignorance. It calls for a shift in focus toward recognizing the presence of racial absences, distortions, and silences. Addressing ignorance is essential for achieving social and cognitive justice, and scholars should be urged to disrupt these structures and promote epistemological diversity.

Focus on ignorance, particularly in racial contexts, may inhibit the development of cultural intelligence (CQ) knowledge. CQ knowledge involves understanding different cultural norms, values, and social practices, which is hindered when ignorance is perpetuated and knowledge is deliberately obscured. Without confronting and dismantling the systems that promote ignorance, individuals and institutions will struggle to develop the awareness and understanding necessary for true cultural intelligence.

One of the primary ways people develop prejudice is by observing social cues and the behaviors of others. Biases often spread and take root this way, as individuals unconsciously mimic the attitudes and actions of those around them (Rojas, 2024). Interestingly, this is the same process through which CQ knowledge can be cultivated. Just as observing others can lead to adopting prejudiced behaviors, it can foster understanding and adaptability in diverse cultural settings. Both processes emphasize the power of observation in shaping perceptions, but they lead to very different outcomes.

Biases can perpetuate inequality. However, CQ knowledge leverages observational learning to promote engagement with different cultures. We can reinforce harmful stereotypes or develop a deeper understanding of cultural norms by observing how people interact within various social groups. Both prejudice and CQ knowledge can spread through similar mechanisms, but where bias contributes to social inequality, CQ knowledge aims to bridge divides and promote inclusivity.

Even when people know stereotypes, they can still fall into biased behaviors. CQ knowledge plays a vital role here by enhancing cultural awareness and encouraging a deeper understanding of cultural differences. By consciously applying cultural intelligence, individuals can counteract the unconscious spread of bias, leading to more effective cross-cultural interactions.

Groups facing bias may become overly sensitive to potential discrimination, though research suggests detecting discrimination is unclear. Prejudice is often subtle, not overt, making it difficult to recognize. Developing CQ knowledge can help marginalized individuals cope with these challenges by fostering resilience against bias. Self-affirmation, a practice where individuals reinforce their core values, can reduce prejudice by lowering defensiveness in the face of perceived threats. Research shows that affirming values leads to more positive intergroup attitudes and cultural norms such as collectivism or individualism influences the success of these interventions. Exploring how self-affirmation affects prejudice across different social contexts could yield valuable insights.

CQ knowledge helps people reframe out-group (actions and attitudes directed toward those perceived as outside of one's own group) behaviors, reducing defensive reactions and scapegoating. By expanding cultural awareness, individuals are less likely to lean on stereotypes when dealing with intergroup (actions, attitudes, and tendencies that occur within a group of individuals who identify as part of the same social category or share a common identity) conflicts, ultimately promoting a more respectful, prejudice-free environment. In the ever-evolving landscape of human interaction, CQ knowledge emerges as a vital tool for those who face prejudice. This understanding acts as a psychological shield, helping individuals navigate the complexities of biased treatment with resilience and grace.

When people immerse themselves in studying diverse cultures, they begin to dismantle the stereotypes and simplistic judgments that often cloud perceptions. This engagement with different cultural contexts is not merely an academic exercise but a transformative journey that sharpens their ability to empathize. By exploring the rich tapestry of global traditions, individuals develop a more nuanced view of others, seeing beyond superficial differences to appreciate each culture's depth and diversity. As their CQ knowledge deepens, individuals find their capacity for empathy greatly enhanced. They learn to see situations from the perspectives of others, fostering a greater understanding and reducing the sting of negative bias. This empathetic approach enables them to navigate social interactions with heightened awareness and compassion.

Furthermore, CQ knowledge encourages critical thinking, and challenges preconceived notions about different cultures. Individuals cultivate a more open and accepting worldview by questioning previously held assumptions and unraveling prejudiced thinking. They understand that cultural differences are not threats but opportunities for connection and growth. In the face of prejudice, CQ knowledge provides a robust defense. It equips individuals with the resilience needed to confront and cope with biased treatment. With a deep understanding of cultural diversity, they approach challenges with a fortified spirit and a compassionate heart, demonstrating the profound impact of cultural intelligence in overcoming prejudice. By enhancing cross-cultural understanding and reducing defensiveness, CQ knowledge helps individuals engage with others openly and respectfully, offering a powerful antidote to the effects of prejudice.

Ethnocentrism Rejects CQ Knowledge

"My dad can beat up your dad" was a common childhood taunt, one of many variations that highlighted competitive comparisons. As children, we often measured our worth by comparing family members, echoing insecurities that persisted into adulthood. A saying I once heard rings true: "Your candle does not burn any brighter by trying to snuff out someone else's." This behavior reflects what psychologist Alfred Adler termed the "superiority complex," characterized by exaggerated claims of accomplishment, dismissing others' opinions, and overcompensating for perceived inadequacies. These patterns often arise from deep-seated insecurity. The superiority complex often reveals itself in subtle yet telling ways: a constant need to compare oneself to others, an inflated sense of one's own abilities, and a propensity to engage only in situations where success seems assured. Those gripped by this complex might dismiss the contributions of others, placing undue value on their own achievements, all the while concealing a deep-seated fear of inadequacy. While not inherently detrimental, ethnocentrism takes this sense of superiority a step further. It is not merely a matter of cultural pride or patriotism but rather the belief in the inherent superiority of one's own culture over others. This perspective can confine individuals to a narrow worldview, like living in an insular bubble where only one's cultural norms and values sway.

Ethnocentrism is a pervasive force that shapes social interactions across the globe, rooted in the belief that one's own cultural group is superior to others. This belief often leads to prejudice and a lack of empathy toward those perceived as different. However, the manifestation of ethnocentrism is intricate and varies widely among different cultural contexts. Research reveals that cultures emphasizing individualism prioritize direct communication and personal decision-making, whereas collectivistic cultures value group consensus and implicit communication. This emphasis on group identity in collectivistic cultures can sometimes foster higher levels of ethnocentrism, as individuals tie their sense of self closely to their cultural group. However, such broad generalizations are not always accurate. The assumption that collectivistic cultures are inherently more ethnocentric than individualistic ones has been challenged by various studies, which uncover a more nuanced reality. For example, students from some collectivistic cultures may show lower levels of ethnocentrism than their individualistic peers, while students from other collectivistic cultures might exhibit higher ethnocentrism.

To truly grasp these variations, one must consider CQ knowledge, which involves a deeper understanding of cultural differences and similarities. CQ knowledge allows individuals to move beyond simplistic cultural models and appreciate the complex factors influencing attitudes and behaviors. Factors such as social environment and educational opportunities significantly shape ethnocentrism and intercultural communication willingness. This underscores the importance of cultivating a nuanced, contextual understanding of cultures rather than relying on broad categorizations.

Ethnocentrism can cast a formidable shadow over intercultural communication, particularly in diverse and multicultural settings. Those who harbor ethnocentric views are often hesitant, if not resistant, to engage with individuals from different cultural backgrounds.

This reluctance can stifle meaningful exchanges, fostering misunderstandings and deepening divisions. However, the impact of ethnocentrism on communication is not uniform; it varies across different cultural landscapes and is influenced by unique experiences and environments. For example, students in urban settings, where intercultural interactions are more frequent, often demonstrate lower levels of ethnocentrism and greater openness to cross-cultural communication. These observations underscore the transformative power of CQ knowledge. CQ knowledge encourages a more open and adaptable mindset by enhancing our understanding of cultural dynamics and their impact on behavior. This shift promotes more effective and meaningful engagement with diverse groups, dismantling the barriers erected by ethnocentrism. However, nurturing this knowledge requires carefully exploring the complexities within cultural contexts. No single model can capture the full richness of human interactions across cultures. Instead, cultivating an awareness of cultural diversity—understanding the intricate factors that shape individual attitudes—lays the foundation for more authentic and impactful intercultural communication. In navigating this journey toward improved communication, CQ knowledge acts as a beacon, guiding individuals through the intricate web of cultural differences. It empowers them to rise above stereotypes and assumptions, fostering deeper connections and a shared understanding.

Valueless

It was bewildering to witness how my grandparents, relatives, and even random Black individuals in my community would go out of their way to accommodate White people, many of whom were far from kind. The contrast was striking and, at times, deeply unsettling. My mother, for instance, worked with employers who openly spoke about Black people using slurs, referring to them as "niggers." However, she remained in their service, navigating the harsh realities of her environment with a quiet resilience.

The dissonance did not stop there. The world outside my family echoed the same contradictions. I would see images of Black people on various store brands, always smiling, always exuding warmth and servitude, even though their roles as servants hardly seemed worthy of such joy. It was as if their happiness was expected despite the degrading circumstances surrounding them.

In the era of Aunt Jemima ads, a nostalgic image of a simpler time was presented, subtly reflecting deeply entrenched racial hierarchies. These advertisements romanticized an era when middle-class White housewives could no longer afford Black maids yet still longed for the warmth and care these women once provided. The message was clear: though Aunt Jemima could no longer be present in the kitchen, her recipe was available—and that, they claimed, was the next best thing. This messaging reduced the humanity of Black individuals to a mere recipe, a smile, and a service while ignoring the harsh realities and struggles they faced. It was a gentle reminder of a world where racial divisions were quietly maintained, and the contributions of Black people were commodified.

This narrative of racial stereotypes extended beyond advertising into news media. African Americans were often portrayed as criminals or as living in poverty. However, the intensity of these portrayals shifted depending on the context, such as coverage focused on families, athletes, or broader economic conditions (Dixon et al., 2019).

Latinos, largely underrepresented in the media, were frequently associated with illegal immigration, often cast as a threat or as criminals. Meanwhile, White individuals were depicted in a much more favorable light, overrepresented as innocent victims or heroic figures, such as law enforcement officers.

These mediated stereotypes shape public perceptions through repeated exposure, a concept supported by social categorization theory, social identity theory, and priming. For example, the pervasive stereotypes of Black laziness, criminality, athleticism, or promiscuity are embraced by heavy media consumers. Similarly, Latinos, though underrepresented, are often stereotyped as impoverished, criminal, or undocumented, which further reinforces negative perceptions.

When educators address these stereotypes in the classroom, they often encounter questions about why the media perpetuates them. Two prominent explanations arise. The first is that media creators often unconsciously reflect their biases, resulting in an "ethnic blame discourse." Since media producers are predominantly White, this discourse often manifests in content that subtly blames societal problems on ethnic minorities, particularly Black and Latino communities (Dixon et al., 2019).

The second explanation lies in the structural and economic pressures of the media industry. News agencies are driven by profit, and stereotypes offer a simple, easily digestible way to present information that attracts and retains audiences. By relying on stereotypes, media companies ensure higher ratings and, in turn, greater profits. Despite skepticism about these explanations, mediated stereotypes remain pervasive, and digital media amplify their impact. As these stereotypes continue to saturate the media landscape, their effects on public perception and societal attitudes grow even more profound.

In light of these pervasive media representations, it becomes crucial to examine the historical roots of these stereotypes, tracing them back to the era of slavery in the United States. The enduring legacies of slavery have deeply influenced how race and ethnicity are constructed and perceived, both in media and society at large. Understanding these origins allows us to see how deeply ingrained these narratives are, shaping how people of color are depicted and how they are treated and understood in everyday life.

Slavery in America laid the foundation for the systemic racism that persists today. Enslaved Africans were brought to the New World not as humans but as property, their identities reduced to labor and their value measured by their productivity. This dehumanization created a framework where Black individuals were seen not as people but as commodities, a mindset that would reverberate for centuries.

The institution of slavery fostered a hierarchy where White supremacy was normalized and reinforced through laws, customs, and economic practices. This hierarchy justified the brutal treatment of Black people, portraying them as inherently inferior and thus deserving of their subjugation. This narrative, deeply embedded in the American psyche, continued to manifest long after the formal end of slavery through Reconstruction, Jim Crow laws, and the civil rights struggles of the twentieth century.

Even after emancipation, the myth of Black inferiority persisted, reinforcing the belief that Black people were suited only for menial labor or servitude—an idea that found its way into advertisements like those of Aunt Jemima and news portrayals of Black criminality and poverty. This reduction of Black identity to servitude and inferiority not only justified slavery but also laid the groundwork for the stereotypes that continue to permeate media and society.

By examining slavery and its aftermath, we gain a clearer understanding of how these stereotypes were born, how they evolved, and why they remain so difficult to dismantle. The legacy of slavery casts a long shadow over present-day race relations, with its echoes still heard in the stories told by the media, in public policy, and the everyday lives of marginalized communities.

Slavery is a concept so difficult to fathom that, unless you lived within a society where it was a socioeconomic reality, its acceptance seems incomprehensible. How could anyone tolerate the dehumanization and abuse of another human being simply because they were born into unfortunate circumstances? However, during the age of chattel slavery, this was not only tolerated but was woven into the fabric of everyday life. It was not that people universally believed it was morally right, but rather that it aligned with the values and understanding held by those in power within that society. The reality of slavery became an unquestioned norm because it fit within the established socioeconomic order.

As the nation hurtled toward the Civil War, these values solidified into opposing ideologies. The North and South were divided by geography and the deeply rooted core values each region held. Both regions' economic, political, and social structures reflected these divides, contributing to an increasingly hostile environment that compromise alone could not mend.

The North, for example, embraced industrialization and modernization. It was a region of rapid growth driven by manufacturing, infrastructure development, and urbanization. Abolitionist movements gained momentum here, as many in the North viewed slavery as an inhumane institution that needed to be eradicated. They valued human rights and were motivated by a vision of a unified nation under a strong, centralized federal government. The preservation of the Union was paramount, and their nationalism was tied to the idea of progress and industrial power.

The South, however, held fast to its agrarian economy, which relied on plantation-based agriculture and the production of cash crops such as cotton and tobacco. Southerners championed states' rights and valued local governance, pushing back against what they perceived as federal overreach. Their way of life depended on maintaining a traditional social order that included a rigid hierarchy, with slavery at its foundation. For them, the fight was about preserving their culture, economy, and autonomy.

These conflicting values starkly contrasted priorities and lifestyles between the North and South. The North's vision of progress and unity clashed with the South's desire to uphold its agricultural traditions and self-governance. Understanding these deeply entrenched values helps explain the motivations and actions of both sides during this pivotal period in American history.

The Civil War erupted because the divisions ran too deep for a peaceful resolution. It is a stark reminder of the catastrophic consequences that can arise when a nation becomes so profoundly divided.

Slavery and the broader conflict that led to the Civil War cannot be fully understood without considering the value systems that shaped people's beliefs, behaviors, and actions during that era. A value system is a set of principles or ideals that drive an individual or society's decisions, priorities, and ways of living. In the case of the North and South, their opposing value systems underpinned the deep divide that led to one of the most defining conflicts in American history.

In the South, the value system was heavily rooted in tradition, and the preservation of a way of life passed down through generations.

FINDING CULTURAL ACUITY

This agrarian society placed a high value on land, agriculture, and a social hierarchy that reinforced the economic structure dependent on slavery. Slavery was not just an economic necessity but also a social institution that upheld the South's rigid social order. Within this value system, states' rights were paramount, as local governance was seen as the best protector of their cultural norms and economic interests. For many Southerners, federal interference was viewed as a threat to their entire way of life.

Conversely, the North's value system revolved around progress, innovation, and industrialization. The rapid growth of manufacturing and infrastructure transformed the North into a bustling hub of modernity. Values such as human rights and abolitionism gained traction, leading many Northerners to view slavery as not only a moral wrong but a backward institution that hindered the nation's progress. Their commitment to a strong centralized government reflected their belief in national unity and the collective progress of the country as a whole.

The divergence in value systems created an unbridgeable chasm between the North and South. Each side saw the other as fundamentally incompatible with their way of life. To the North, the South's dependence on slavery was an affront to human dignity and a barrier to modernization. To the South, the North's push for industrialization and centralized control threatened their autonomy and traditional values. The conflict over slavery was, at its core, a clash of value systems that extended far beyond economics—it was about what each side believed was the right way to live, govern, and move forward as a nation.

This is a powerful reminder of how deeply embedded value systems can shape the direction of entire societies. When groups hold fundamentally different values, compromise becomes difficult, if not impossible. The Civil War is a stark example of what happens when value systems collide, leaving little room for understanding or negotiation. The battle lines were drawn not just over slavery but over the very principles that guided how people saw the world, their place in it, and the future they envisioned for their country.

In many ways, this clash of value systems is a recurring theme in history. When values are deeply ingrained, they can blind people to alternative perspectives, leading to conflicts that are difficult to resolve. Understanding these underlying value systems is crucial for making sense of historical events and, perhaps, for finding ways to navigate similar divisions in the future.

CQ knowledge is the ability to deeply understand and appreciate the cultural norms, practices, and values that shape how people from diverse backgrounds think, communicate, and behave. In an increasingly interconnected world, CQ knowledge is crucial in helping individuals navigate and respect the rich tapestry of values across cultures. This understanding is about learning facts or behaviors and grasping the underlying value systems that guide how individuals and groups make sense of the world.

At the heart of CQ knowledge lies the concept of value systems. A value system is a set of deeply held principles that shape people's beliefs, decisions, and actions. These systems are often embedded within cultural contexts, passed down through generations, and form the foundation of how people perceive their place in the world. They influence everything from family dynamics to work ethics, social interactions, and conflict resolution strategies. To truly understand another culture, one must recognize that different cultures prioritize different values, leading to varied approaches to life, relationships, and problem-solving.

For example, take the Amish community. Many may not wish to adopt the Amish way of life, yet their value system—rooted in simplicity, hard work, and community—offers much to admire. The Amish value traditional lifestyles, which contribute to their exceptional health outcomes. With much lower rates of diseases like cancer, largely due to their active and health-conscious way of life, they demonstrate the benefits of living in alignment with their values. Their dedication to avoiding sloth and idleness, as guided by their religious beliefs, translates into a culture known for its diligence and skilled craftsmanship. This example illustrates how CQ knowledge allows individuals to respect and even appreciate values that differ from their own, enabling them to engage more thoughtfully with other cultures.

Those who have developed a strong CQ knowledge know the diversity of values that inform people's behaviors and attitudes across cultures. For instance, someone with high CQ knowledge understands that in some cultures, respect for elders and authority is a central value, while in others, questioning authority is seen as a sign of intellectual curiosity and engagement. This awareness prevents the misinterpretation of behaviors that might otherwise seem strange or inappropriate. It also fosters better communication, as individuals can tailor their interactions to align with the values of those they are engaging with.

Moreover, CQ knowledge provides a deeper understanding of how value systems impact decision-making processes. In hierarchical cultures, for example, leaders or elders often make decisions with the expectation that others will follow without question. In contrast, more egalitarian cultures may prioritize democratic decision-making, seeking input from various voices. CQ knowledge equips individuals to navigate these differences effectively, ensuring they approach decision-making in ways that respect the cultural context.

Recognizing the potential tensions between value systems is another key aspect of CQ knowledge. Sometimes, these value systems can clash, leading to misunderstandings or conflicts. For example, a Western businessperson who values direct communication might find themselves at odds with a colleague from a culture that prioritizes indirect communication and saving face. Without CQ's knowledge, this situation could lead to frustration or even a breakdown in communication. However, someone with a well-developed understanding of different cultural value systems would recognize the underlying reasons for the indirect communication and adjust their approach accordingly.

CQ knowledge also helps individuals adapt to local norms and practices. By understanding the value systems that underlie cultural behaviors, people can better adapt their own behavior when interacting in different cultural contexts. This adaptability allows them to adjust their expectations and actions in ways that foster more harmonious interactions and build stronger, more respectful relationships across cultures.

Ultimately, CQ knowledge is about more than just learning the facts of other cultures; it's about cultivating a deep understanding of the values that drive those cultures. With this knowledge, individuals can engage more meaningfully with people from diverse backgrounds, appreciating the richness of different ways of life while fostering a sense of connection and mutual respect.

The reflections on mediated stereotypes, historical narratives of slavery, and the enduring clash of value systems provide a rich backdrop for understanding the importance of cultural intelligence (CQ) in today's world. CQ knowledge— the capacity to comprehend and respect diverse cultural norms, practices, and values—offers a way to bridge the divides created by history, media, and societal structures. By cultivating CQ knowledge, individuals can navigate these complex landscapes with empathy, insight, and a deeper appreciation for the diverse value systems that shape human behavior.

At its core, CQ knowledge involves recognizing that value systems are not universal but are deeply rooted in cultural contexts. These systems guide how people interpret the world, form relationships, and make decisions. They are shaped by history, religion, socioeconomic conditions, and shared experiences. For example, the legacy of slavery in the United States did more than exploit labor—it established and reinforced a hierarchy of values that prioritized White supremacy while devaluing Black lives. These entrenched value systems justified systemic oppression and continue to influence societal attitudes, as seen in the lingering stereotypes perpetuated by media representations.

Yet, CQ knowledge goes beyond merely identifying these disparities; it equips individuals to understand the "why" behind behaviors and attitudes. It allows us to contextualize the resilience of Black communities, like those in my own experience, who often navigated systemic inequities with strength and dignity. The quiet resilience of my mother, who endured a workplace filled with blatant racism, reflects not just personal fortitude but also a cultural value system that prioritized perseverance, adaptability, and the survival of the family. CQ knowledge invites us to honor these values while recognizing the broader forces that demand such resilience.

Moreover, CQ knowledge sheds light on how different societies approach values such as individualism versus collectivism, authority versus egalitarianism, or tradition versus progress. For example, understanding the Amish community's emphasis on simplicity, community, and hard work provides a window into a way of life vastly different from the mainstream, yet profoundly aligned with their cultural and religious values. By examining these differences, we can appreciate how value systems shape behaviors, from health practices to conflict resolution, while also learning from those differences to enhance our own perspectives.

In connecting CQ knowledge to values development, it becomes clear that engaging with other cultures is not just about understanding the "other"—it is also a pathway to reflecting on and evolving our own values. Intercultural experiences often challenge the assumptions we hold about what is "right" or "normal," encouraging us to consider alternative ways of thinking and living. This process of reflection and adaptation is crucial for personal growth, as it fosters a more nuanced and flexible worldview.

For instance, exposure to hierarchical cultures where respect for elders and authority is paramount can prompt those from egalitarian societies to reconsider the value they place on experience and wisdom. Conversely, individuals from hierarchical societies may learn to appreciate the benefits of democratic dialogue and individual expression. Through this exchange, value systems are not necessarily abandoned but enriched, creating a more comprehensive framework for navigating an interconnected world.

CQ knowledge also plays a critical role in addressing the tensions that arise when value systems clash. Misunderstandings rooted in cultural differences can lead to frustration, conflict, or even perpetuation of harmful stereotypes. However, with a well-developed understanding of diverse cultural values, individuals can approach these situations with greater sensitivity and adaptability. Whether it's recognizing the importance of saving face in indirect communication or understanding the historical context of mistrust in certain communities, CQ knowledge enables more effective and respectful interactions.

As the world becomes increasingly interconnected, the development of CQ knowledge is not just an asset but a necessity. It empowers individuals to transcend cultural boundaries, fostering mutual respect and collaboration in ways that were once unimaginable. At the same time, it challenges us to confront the biases and value systems that have shaped our own lives, offering an opportunity for growth and transformation.

Enduring stereotypes, historical injustices, and deeply entrenched value systems explored in this chapter underscore the importance of CQ knowledge as a tool for bridging divides and building a more inclusive society. By engaging with the diverse values that shape human behavior, we not only enhance our understanding of others but also cultivate the empathy, adaptability, and wisdom needed to navigate the complexities of the modern world. The journey toward cultural intelligence is ultimately a journey toward deeper human connection, allowing us to honor the past, challenge the present, and envision a more equitable future.

Reflection Questions

Chapter Seven

I. Can learning the cultural frameworks of others help reduce unconscious bias and increase cultural sensitivity?

II. Why do you think understanding the values and norms of different cultures can improve your ability to navigate cross-cultural interactions effectively? Are there examples in your past experiences that would support this?

III. How do historical and social contexts enhance CQ knowledge?

CHAPTER EIGHT

CQ STRATEGY: SEE NO EVIL, HEAR NO EVIL, SPEAK NO EVIL

Intelligence Strategy

Despite being placed in advanced and gifted-student classes throughout my K-12 years, I never saw myself as particularly intelligent. Instead, I often questioned how I ended up there. I worked hard and was determined to be a good student, but some subjects remained elusive, particularly mathematics. Reflecting, my greatest challenge was not merely the content but my ability to focus. My mind was always darting from one thought to another, racing down rabbit trails of imagination just as I tried to concentrate on the lesson.

However, something shifted when the schoolwork involved creative problem-solving tasks. In those moments, my mind came alive, effortlessly connecting ideas in ways that felt both intuitive and freeing. I also noticed that when a teacher approached subjects conceptually—breaking down the material into ideas rather than rote formulas—the lessons clicked more easily for me. It was as if my mind was primed to work with concepts, to mold and shape ideas rather than memorize information.

This personal experience is an example of cultural intelligence (CQ) strategy. CQ strategy involves recognizing one's cognitive approach to different cultural settings, planning for diverse interactions, and adjusting behavior based on ongoing reflections. Much like how I discovered conceptual teaching resonated more with me, the CQ strategy encourages individuals to identify and adapt their mental frameworks in cross-cultural contexts. By acknowledging how different approaches to learning impacted my ability to engage with the material, I can apply this awareness in cultural scenarios, seeking out the conceptual "language" of another culture and using creative problem-solving to bridge gaps in understanding. Recognizing these personal learning patterns highlights the importance of being metacognitively aware, allowing me to adjust strategies in both academic and cultural situations.

CQ strategy, or metacognitive CQ, is critical in navigating the complexities of culturally diverse environments. This element of cultural intelligence involves individuals' mental processes to understand and make sense of their experiences during cross-cultural interactions. CQ strategy can be seen as a mental framework that guides how a person plans for, engages with, and reflects on these encounters.

The first step in CQ strategy is planning. Before engaging in a multicultural situation, individuals with high CQ strategy approach the interaction thoughtfully. They consider potential cultural differences, social norms, communication styles, and even taboos that may come into play. This preparation enables them to anticipate challenges and develop strategies to address them effectively, setting the stage for a more sensitive and productive exchange.

Awareness is the next vital component of the CQ strategy. During the interaction, these individuals maintain a heightened sense of mindfulness. They are attentive to spoken words and nonverbal cues that often convey deeper meaning, such as body language, tone, and gestures. This continuous monitoring of both their behaviors and the cultural cues of others allows them to remain adaptable, adjusting their approach as needed to fit the cultural context. This flexibility is essential in fostering mutual understanding and respect.

After the interaction, reflection becomes key. People with high CQ strategies take time to evaluate their performance. They assess what went well, what challenges arose, and how they might improve in future interactions. This reflective practice helps deepen their cultural intelligence, enabling them to learn from each experience and refine their approach to cross-cultural encounters. By actively engaging in this reflective process, they enhance their ability to interpret cultural cues accurately and respond effectively.

Individuals who develop strong CQ strategies are skilled at navigating cultural differences and managing conflicts that may emerge from misunderstandings. Their ability to assess their thought processes and those of others empowers them to respond with greater insight and accuracy. This capability not only fosters effective communication but also promotes the building of stronger, more inclusive relationships with people from diverse backgrounds.

By cultivating CQ strategy through planning, awareness, and reflection, individuals can improve communication across cultures, resolve conflicts more effectively, and build deeper, meaningful relationships. The journey to high CQ strategy requires ongoing effort, but the benefits—enhanced understanding, better relationships, and greater inclusivity—make it an essential skill in today's increasingly interconnected world.

Thinking about Thinking

In the intricate landscape of cognitive science, metacognition is a profound concept, often described as "thinking about thinking." It is the ability to monitor, regulate, and control one's cognitive processes, and it plays a pivotal role in learning, education, and overall cognitive development. The literature overflows with attempts to sharpen executive function (EF) components, such as inhibitory control, attention shifting, and working memory, each crucial to the broader spectrum of cognitive growth.

While not a direct measure of metacognition, working memory has been a focal point in training designed to boost cognitive abilities and academic performance. However, despite the promise, research findings are mixed. Many meta-analyses highlight that cognitive training yields only modest and short-lived improvements in cognitive control. However, one study revealed that training children on EF components like working memory, inhibitory control, and cognitive flexibility improved the same domains. These gains, unfortunately, did not translate to far-transfer effects—skills in one domain did not improve others. The research in adults suggests a more promising outlook, with some studies reporting both near- and far-transfer effects following EF training. On a neural level, a fascinating discovery emerged: cognitive training appeared to reduce brain activity in regions typically associated with externally focused attention. This indicated that training might ease the demands on such attention, allowing the brain to work more efficiently.

Training has shown promising results in meta-knowledge—knowledge about one's cognitive processes. Studies have found that individuals who receive feedback on their metacognitive judgments, such as in perceptual decision-making tasks, enhance their metacognitive accuracy. Notably, this improvement extends to untrained tasks as well. Further exploration into mindfulness meditation reveals that just two weeks of training can bolster meta-knowledge in memory tasks, a change possibly linked to structural changes in the brain—specifically, increased gray matter density in the anterior prefrontal cortex (aPFC).

As we delve deeper into the mechanisms of metacognition, it becomes clear that this complex process is studied through various lenses, from metacognitive judgments to executive function tasks. The distinctions between metacognitive sensitivity, bias, and efficacy are central to understanding how individuals evaluate their performance. While executive function is often seen as an online process—operating swiftly without much reflective thought—metacognitive judgments are viewed as offline processes that require deeper reflection and meta-representation.

Interestingly, research has identified a network of brain regions consistently involved in metacognitive tasks. Though activated differently depending on context, these regions play a crucial role in meta-knowledge and meta-control. Training in metacognition, especially in offline tasks involving self-reflection, has shown promise in creating structural changes in these regions, indicating that the metacognitive network in the brain is malleable.

However, despite these promising findings, a significant gap remains in the ecological validity of metacognition research. How well do these laboratory findings translate to real-life scenarios? Can an individual who excels in judging their performance in controlled tasks also accurately assess their performance in more complex real-world situations, such as during an exam or daily learning? Bridging this gap is essential for advancing our understanding of metacognition and its practical implications.

This is where the CQ strategy comes into play. CQ strategy, the metacognitive aspect of cultural intelligence, involves planning, awareness, and checking in cross-cultural contexts. Just as metacognition helps individuals monitor and regulate their thinking, CQ strategy enables individuals to navigate diverse cultural environments by reflecting on their cultural knowledge and adjusting their approach. Integrating the CQ strategy into metacognitive training could enhance individuals' abilities to apply their cognitive skills in culturally diverse real-world settings, making metacognition more relevant and effective in everyday life.

The Cupper Sisters' Epiphany

In grade school, there is always that one child—the scapegoat, the one used by others to elevate their own social standing, to carve out a niche in the fragile hierarchy of the playground. More often than not, I found myself taking turns in that role. But I was not innocent either. I, too, was guilty of joining the pack and participating in the cruelty, as I vividly recall from an incident in first grade.

Being only a couple of years apart, my brothers and I often attended the same school. Here, we first encountered the Cupper sisters—twins notorious for their eccentric clothing and bizarre reputation. Everyone knew them, though not fondly. They were an oddity, their presence a spectacle that drew both ridicule and uneasy fascination.

The Cupper sisters were not treated kindly. There was an unspoken ritual among the students: if you saw them, you were supposed to pinch them and run. It was a cruel game, but none of us understood the weight of our actions. We were young, barely aware of right and wrong. Our moral compass had not yet aligned with empathy.

My brothers would come home with stories—schoolyard legends that revolved around these girls. They would say that the sisters would retaliate if you provoked them and were fierce in their defense. This only fueled the mystique around them, making the idea of pinching them more thrilling and dangerous. It was not just about the pinch but about proving something to the group.

The legend went further, claiming the Cupper sisters had the worst case of cooties anyone could imagine. To be touched by them, even briefly, was seen as a kind of social death. The way they dressed did not help their case either. In hindsight, their attire was not so odd as it was out of fashion. Perhaps their clothes were chosen by an older parent or grandparent who took pride in how they presented the girls to the world. But to us, they seemed stuck in another time.

Each day, they arrived at school in white or black patent leather shoes, ankle-high bobby socks with eyelet lace tops, and plaid pinafore dresses. Over this, they wore white cardigan sweaters, always buttoned at the top and draped over their shoulders like capes. And then there were the barrettes—countless colorful barrettes clipped into their short brown hair as if trying to brighten their world with a rainbow of plastic. They were never seen without their white gloves, pristine and out of place amid the rough and tumble of the playground.

The day came when I could not avoid it any longer. It was my turn. Do or die, I had to pinch one of the Cupper sisters. It did not matter which one. My heart raced as the gang watched me from a distance, waiting for me to prove myself. I spied them out in the schoolyard and zeroed in on the nearest sister. I ran toward her, hand extended, ready to fulfill the ritual.

But before I could reach her, one of the sisters spun around startlingly. She locked eyes with me, daring me to pinch her. "You better not!" she said. At that moment, I froze. Her challenge hung in the air, and I realized I could not do it. I turned and ran, abandoning the mission, my heart pounding. Perhaps it was the first time I truly understood the weight of what we were doing—the cruelty of it all.

When I failed to go through with the ritual of pinching the Cupper sisters, my standing among my so-called friends at school took a nosedive. Overnight, I found myself shamed and socially isolated. It felt like punishment at the time, but looking back, I realize it was a turning point—a blessing in disguise. The experience forced me to confront my own behavior, and it dawned on me that I never truly wanted to hurt anyone in the first place.

In retrospect, the Cupper sisters' appearance did not seem odd to me at all. Their clothing, while different, had a certain charm that intrigued me more than it repelled. Moreover, if they did have cooties, perhaps I did not mind. What stood out to me the most was how they were always there for each other, supporting one another amid the relentless cruelty of the other children. They did not seem strange to me; they seemed resilient. I began to admire them far more than I ever considered them odd.

More importantly, the incident sparked a deep reflection within me. I realized I did not want to be that person—the one who joined the pack to bully others just to fit in. After thinking long and hard, I saw that what everyone was saying about the sisters was not true. They were not the monsters they were made out to be; they were quite nice. From that moment on, I vowed never to participate in such cruelty again.

It was a transformative experience that planted the seeds of humility within me. For the first time, I understood that I did not have to follow the crowd. I could choose to be different, to be kinder. That realization has stayed with me ever since.

Humility: The Ultimate Culturally Intelligent Strategy

Humility is the cornerstone of cultural intelligence, weaving its influence through CQ drive, CQ knowledge, and CQ strategy. At its core, humility is about recognizing one's limitations, embracing the idea that learning is a lifelong process, and genuinely valuing the perspectives of others. It nurtures a learner's mindset, which is essential for navigating and adapting to the complexities of diverse cultures. This openness transforms interactions into meaningful and respectful exchanges, fostering genuine understanding across cultural divides.

Within CQ strategy, humility is pivotal in inviting flexibility in thought and planning. It encourages reflective thinking—an opportunity to assess one's assumptions and confront inherent biases. This reflective process allows individuals to adapt their approach, continuously refining their strategies based on feedback and new insights. Humility makes cultural strategies dynamic rather than rigid, allowing them to evolve in response to new information.

Researchers refer to intellectual humility as acknowledging that one's beliefs may be flawed. It is an understanding that personal knowledge is incomplete and that opinions, often shaped by psychological biases, can be based on limited or faulty evidence. When intellectual humility is absent, ignorance can manifest as prejudice. Humility is not just a personal virtue but a critical safeguard against the ignorance that fuels cultural misunderstandings. While practicing intellectual humility will not eliminate bias, it helps us become more aware of our knowledge limitations. This awareness can act as a buffer, softening some of our authoritarian, dogmatic, and biased tendencies and fostering a more open-minded and balanced approach to understanding others (Porter et al.; Grossmann, 2022).

According to Porter et al. (2022), intellectual humility, though related to general humility, modesty, perspective-taking, and open-mindedness, is a distinct concept centered on recognizing the limits of one's knowledge. While general humility involves how people view their strengths and weaknesses across various aspects of life, intellectual humility specifically addresses awareness of one's intellectual limitations. Modesty, on the other hand, is more about social awareness and the desire to avoid attention. In contrast, intellectual humility is rooted in acknowledging one's ignorance and the fallibility of one's thinking. Perspective-taking involves understanding and recognizing others' points of view, while intellectual humility focuses on recognizing potential flaws or limitations in one's perspective. Open-mindedness, often linked to intellectual humility, involves a fair and unbiased consideration of differing viewpoints. However, open-mindedness does not necessarily mean recognizing the limitations of one's knowledge. Though related to these other concepts, intellectual humility has its unique place, with multiple definitions reflecting its diverse applications across different fields.

With deep philosophical roots, intellectual humility is often viewed as the delicate balance between intellectual arrogance—overestimating one's beliefs—and intellectual diffidence—undervaluing them. Inspired by Aristotle's concept of the Golden Mean, intellectual humility is seen as a virtue that adapts to the demands of each situation. However, because circumstances vary, this virtue remains dynamic and situationally sensitive, and the same traits attributed to intellectual humility may not always be considered virtuous in every context (Porter et al. 2022).

Psychological scientists offer various interpretations of intellectual humility. Some see it as a form of metacognition, where individuals reflect on their beliefs and recognize the limitations of their knowledge. This perspective highlights the fallibility of human understanding, acknowledging that beliefs can be flawed and opinions are often based on incomplete information. Others view intellectual humility as a multidimensional phenomenon, encompassing metacognition and valuing others' beliefs, admitting ignorance or mistakes, and fostering a genuine desire to seek the truth.

Some scholars favor a broader understanding of intellectual humility, and those focus more narrowly on metacognition. Advocates of a broader view argue that intellectual humility should include appreciation for others' insights, behavioral responses to recognizing errors, and the underlying motives for thinking and acting. In contrast, proponents of a metacognitive approach argue that adding too many features can dilute the concept, making it harder to study with precision. They caution that multidimensional measures may blur the clarity of intellectual humility, as individuals may score similarly even if they excel in one area and struggle in another.

Cultural contexts deeply influence how people think and process information, profoundly shaping their intellectual humility. In societies that emphasize interdependence, such as Japan, individuals are more likely to reflect on the thoughts and emotions of others, viewing themselves about their community and relationships. This mindset helps them avoid overlooking important contextual details that might be missed by those in more independent cultures like the USA, where individualism is more prominent. In cultures that prioritize interdependence, people are more attuned to relational goals, social cues, and the nuances of their social environment. Their sense of self is intertwined with their community, leading to a heightened awareness of social context and a greater ability to navigate it thoughtfully. This contrast between interdependent and independent societies highlights culture's role in shaping behavior and how individuals approach knowledge, relationships, and intellectual humility.

Cultural humility is a deep commitment to ongoing self-reflection, challenging power imbalances, and cultivating relationships based on mutual respect to create a more inclusive society. It is concerned with recognizing the limitations of understanding other cultures and identities, involving ongoing learning from others and acknowledging the power imbalances inherent in cross-cultural interactions. This practice goes beyond mere awareness, becoming an active approach that confronts hierarchies, questions organizational policies, and strengthens community capacity. By embedding cultural humility into daily life, individuals and organizations can work to promote social inclusion, especially for those who have been marginalized or excluded

(Chávez, 2021). Cultural humility aims to build more equitable and respectful relationships across cultural boundaries. It moves beyond cultural competence to an ongoing practice of humility, self-critique, and learning.

Intellectual and cultural humility are deeply rooted in openness and self-awareness, yet they differ in focus and application. Intellectual humility is about recognizing the limitations of one's knowledge and beliefs, embracing the fallibility of human understanding, and fostering a genuine desire to seek the truth. It can be seen as metacognition—reflecting on one's thoughts—or as a broader phenomenon that values others' beliefs, admits ignorance, and encourages thoughtful exploration.

Cultural humility, by contrast, is a commitment to recognizing the limitations of one's understanding of other cultures and identities. It involves ongoing self-reflection, learning from others, and confronting power imbalances that often define cross-cultural interactions. This practice extends beyond awareness, actively challenging hierarchies and strengthening community ties to promote social inclusion, particularly for those who have been marginalized.

Intellectual and cultural humility demands openness to new information and perspectives despite their differences. They require individuals to recognize their limitations and approach others with curiosity, respect, and a willingness to learn. In both forms, humility is not a static trait but an ongoing practice that fosters personal growth, understanding, and more equitable relationships across intellectual and cultural divides.

Reflection Questions

Chapter Eight

I. What steps would you take to consistently improve your ability to plan and adapt your interactions in culturally diverse situations?

II. How can you leverage self-awareness and feedback to enhance your cultural intelligence strategy over time?

III. How can you reflect on and adjust your personal biases to develop a more strategic approach when engaging with different cultures?

CHAPTER NINE

CULTURALLY APPROPRIATE ACTIONS

Adapting, We Will Go

The transition from middle school to high school was traumatic in so many ways, but mostly because of my deep-seated social awkwardness. I have never felt particularly significant, but those feelings of inferiority multiplied exponentially on my first day of high school. I was barely fourteen, still teetering on the edge of adolescence, my emotions a mess of postpubescent confusion. High school became a horror show. However, there were some highs, overshadowed mostly by lows.

Not even four months earlier, I had made friends with a group of guys through a summer work program. We worked at an Orthodox Jewish retirement home, where we spent our days learning the value of hard work and developing a strong work ethic. Despite our age, we stayed clear of the typical mischief boys our age usually indulged in. We even bonded over our first paychecks, buying matching shirts to show off our newfound fraternity. Our camaraderie was genuine, though sometimes we could not help but cause some unintentional trouble.

The experience of losing that friendship and the painful realization of my struggles to adapt socially remained a defining moment. It underscored how daunting it can be to navigate unfamiliar territory—whether in high school hallways or broader cultural landscapes. At the time, I did not have the tools to adjust to new social norms or expectations, but years later, I understood these struggles through the lens of *cultural intelligence action or CQ action*. This concept reflects the ability to adapt verbal and nonverbal behaviors to meet the demands of culturally diverse settings.

Unlike default behaviors, which are automatic responses shaped by familiar environments, CQ action requires intentionality. It calls for a deliberate adjustment to one's behavior in response to different cultural norms, fostering effective communication and smoother interactions. This adaptability is not just a social skill; it is a cornerstone of cultural intelligence (CQ), which also includes CQ drive (motivation), CQ knowledge (understanding of cultural norms), and CQ strategy (metacognitive planning). CQ action is the application of these elements in real-world scenarios, enabling individuals to meet the challenges of multicultural settings with grace and efficiency.

Research has shown that CQ action significantly influences decision-making processes. In professional or cross-cultural environments, where assumptions and norms often clash, individuals with high CQ action demonstrate a remarkable ability to pivot. They can adjust their communication style, problem-solving strategies, and negotiation tactics to align with the expectations of diverse groups.

This flexibility enhances both interpersonal relationships and outcomes, particularly in multicultural teams or international business settings. Studies in organizational behavior confirm that those with high CQ action are more effective at navigating complex cultural dynamics, often achieving superior results in collaborative and competitive scenarios.

The power of CQ action lies in its focus on intentionality. It challenges us to step outside our comfort zones, moving beyond instinctive responses to thoughtfully consider the cultural context of our interactions. This level of adaptability does not just lead to better outcomes in professional settings—it fosters genuine connection and mutual respect across cultural boundaries. By developing CQ action, we do not merely adapt; we thrive, learning to navigate diversity with confidence and empathy.

At the heart of CQ action is behavioral adaptability—the skill of fine-tuning your speech, tone, and gestures to align with your cultural context. It is about recognizing when to be more formal, when to loosen up, and how to adjust your demeanor to make others feel comfortable. Imagine walking into a new social setting and instinctively knowing how to present yourself in a way that resonates with the group, whether changing your body language or adjusting how you speak.

Behavioral adaptability refers to adjusting one's behavior to cultural norms and social cues. In the context of CQ, this is a key component of CQ action, which involves an individual's ability to modify verbal and nonverbal actions during cross-cultural interactions appropriately.

Research indicates that behavioral adaptability is essential for successful interactions in diverse cultural environments. Individuals with high CQ action can effectively interpret and respond to cultural cues, leading to better outcomes in international business, negotiations, and personal relationships. For instance, behaviorally adaptable people are more likely to demonstrate flexibility in their communication styles, body language, and social etiquette, allowing them to bridge cultural gaps and build stronger connections.

A study by Ang et al. (2007) highlighted that CQ action is closely linked to performance in multicultural settings, suggesting that individuals who adapt their behaviors tend to perform better in culturally diverse environments. Similarly, research by Imai and Gelfand (2010) demonstrated that CQ action positively influences negotiation outcomes by allowing individuals to tailor their strategies based on the cultural context.

This adaptability is particularly important in today's globalized world, where interactions across cultures are increasingly common. Developing CQ action involves understanding cultural differences and practicing flexibility in behavior to foster effective communication and collaboration.

Communication styles are also central to CQ action. Each culture has its way of expressing ideas, some more direct, others more subtle. Being able to switch between these styles is crucial for effective cross-cultural interactions. It is like learning a new language—not just the words, but the nuances that come with them, understanding when to be straightforward and read between the lines.

But it is not always possible to prepare for every situation where improvisation comes into play. CQ action includes the ability to think on your feet and to modify your behavior in real time when cultural differences demand a quick shift in approach. This is not just about being reactive; it is about being nimble and resourceful and finding ways to adapt without losing yourself. Finally, there is behavioral range—the ability to expand your set of behaviors to fit a variety of cultural settings while still staying true to who you are. This is not about faking it; it is about broadening your comfort zone and learning to engage with people from different backgrounds in ways that feel authentic for you and them.

Cultural Fluency

Understanding and mastering CQ action is not just about cultural fluency; it is about social fluency—the ability to navigate and thrive in any environment, no matter how unfamiliar or challenging. Looking back, I realize that if I had known this back in high school, maybe things would have been different. As a bona fide introvert struggling with social fluency and lacking the confidence to adapt, I often wondered what difference it might have made if I had been equipped with the tools to engage in CQ action.

Both introverts and extroverts can be effective when engaging in CQ action, but their approaches differ significantly due to their inherent personality traits. As an introvert, I often stood on the sidelines, observing and assessing situations before making any moves. This reflective nature is a hallmark of introverts regarding behavioral adaptability. Introverts tend to be more deliberate in adjusting their behavior, excelling in environments where strategic, well-thought-out changes are necessary. By contrast, extroverts are more likely to dive headfirst into social situations, making quicker, more spontaneous adjustments based on the feedback they receive from others. Their natural energy allows them to engage directly with people, adapting on the fly.

Communication styles also reveal these differences. Introverts typically prefer controlled, thoughtful communication. In culturally diverse settings, they may take extra time to process information before responding, ensuring their words are carefully calibrated to the cultural context. They often excel in cultures that value contemplation and restraint. Extroverts, however, are more outgoing and enthusiastic communicators. They can quickly build rapport in cultures that appreciate open and direct communication. However, they may need to temper their style in settings where quietness or reserve is the norm.

Another key component of CQ action is improvisation—the ability to modify behavior in real-time when cultural differences demand a quick shift in strategy. With their preference for planning, introverts may take a more structured approach to improvisation, relying on their foresight to guide them through challenging situations. They often excel in environments that allow for observation before action. Conversely, extroverts are comfortable with in-the-moment changes, using their social instincts to navigate fast-paced cultural interactions where immediate adjustments are needed.

Regarding social interactions, introverts typically prefer fewer but more meaningful connections. They focus on building deep relationships and gaining a thorough understanding of those they interact with, often taking longer to engage fully but doing so with intentionality and focus. Extroverts thrive on numerous social interactions, easily connecting with many people. Their energy and enthusiasm help them engage quickly across different cultures, though they must be mindful not to overwhelm others who value more subdued social interactions.

Finally, behavioral range—the breadth of adaptive behaviors one can employ—is another area where introverts and extroverts differ. Introverts may develop a narrower but deeper range of behaviors, excelling in settings that value listening, contemplation, and deep engagement. Their strength lies in mastering a few key adaptive behaviors and applying them thoughtfully. Extroverts, by contrast, may cultivate a broader behavioral repertoire, experimenting with various approaches to fit different cultural norms. Their comfort in diverse social situations makes them more versatile in their adaptations.

Each personality type brings its strengths and challenges to CQ action. Introverts are reflective, strategic, and thoughtful in adapting their behaviors, excelling in cultures that prioritize introspection and indirect communication. However, they may find it more difficult to adapt to highly dynamic or fast-paced environments and can become drained by too much social interaction, potentially limiting their adaptability. Extroverts are energetic and comfortable in diverse social settings, excelling in cultures that value direct communication and high levels of interaction. However, their spontaneity can sometimes lead to missteps if they do not carefully assess the cultural context.

In the end, both introverts and extroverts can effectively engage in CQ action, though in different ways. Introverts shine when given the space to observe, reflect, and strategically adapt. Extroverts thrive in real-time interactions, quickly adapting their behavior to fit the situation. The key to success lies in leveraging these natural strengths while being mindful of each personality type's challenges in cross-cultural interactions.

In a study conducted by Şahin et al. (2014), researchers set out to explore the influence of international assignments on the development of CQ over time. They wanted to understand whether personality traits, specifically extroversion and openness to experience, played a role in shaping how individuals adapted to different cultures. The study followed participants over six months, revealing that those who engaged in international experiences significantly increased their ability to navigate and understand new cultures.

People with more extroverted personalities showed marked improvements in their ability to think and act appropriately in diverse cultural settings. Their sociable nature and confidence led them to embrace opportunities for cross-cultural interactions, enhancing their adaptability and behavior. On the other hand, individuals with a strong sense of curiosity and openness to new experiences developed a heightened motivation to engage with different cultures. Their willingness to explore and immerse themselves in unfamiliar environments fueled their drive to connect with others across cultural boundaries.

These findings underscore the powerful impact of personality traits on how individuals grow and adapt during international experiences. While extroversion and openness to experience played significant roles, their effects varied, highlighting the complex relationship between personality and cultural adaptability.

Remember Me

Navigating the delicate dance between adaptability and cultural identity is a crucial challenge in cross-cultural interactions. When it comes to CQ action—the ability to adjust one's behavior to fit diverse cultural settings effectively—the task is to blend flexibility with a steadfast commitment to one's cultural values. This balance is essential for fostering genuine and respectful interactions in a multicultural world.

Successfully integrating into a new cultural environment requires more than just superficial adjustments. It demands a deep development of both emotional and cultural intelligence. To truly connect and respond in ways that resonate positively, one must learn to interpret and engage with others from different backgrounds with insight and sensitivity. This nuanced understanding enriches personal interactions and enhances one's ability to positively impact oneself and others globally (Thompson, 2018).

In Thompson's (2018) qualitative phenomenological study on the emotional and cultural intelligence of international students, the researcher uncovered a profound connection between this intelligence and the student's ability to navigate and integrate into the social fabric of a university setting. Through the participants' voices, Thompson illuminated the complex emotions and cultural challenges they encountered during their collegiate journey. The study revealed that those students who developed a deeper understanding of American culture found it easier to integrate socially within the university environment.

Furthermore, the findings underscored the critical role that emotional intelligence plays in this process. Thompson argued that by enhancing one's emotional intelligence, an individual increases their likelihood of being socially engaged and involved. This insight emphasizes the importance for institutions of higher learning, particularly those with diverse international student bodies, to implement social programs that foster emotional and cultural intelligence.

However, as these students adapted to their new surroundings, many experienced a significant shift in their social behavior. While some embraced these changes, others grappled with discomfort and unease. Inherently, there was a risk of losing touch with their cultural identity in their efforts to assimilate and embrace American culture. The tension between adaptation and identity preservation becomes a poignant aspect of cross-cultural engagement, raising critical questions about how one can balance the integration process without sacrificing the essence of who they are.

Integrating into a new society is a lifelong endeavor that intertwines deeply with an immigrant's social connectedness and psychological well-being. Shuang Liu (2017) delves into this complex process, highlighting that successful integration hinges on the relationships immigrants build and their belonging within their new communities. These connections are vital, as they not only foster a sense of inclusion but also protect against the dangers of depression and social isolation that often accompany those who struggle to integrate.

However, the path to cultural integration is far from straightforward. It involves navigating the intricate process of identifying and balancing multiple cultural identities, a challenge that has grown more complex in our increasingly globalized world. Developing a bicultural or multicultural identity is not a static process but one shaped by various cultural and contextual forces that change over time. These forces vary across different local and national settings, and their influence can differ widely depending on the ethnic group and the surrounding mainstream culture.

Liu's work also reveals that belonging to an ethnic or cultural group does not automatically ensure a strong cultural identification. The broader cultural environment shapes how individuals connect with their heritage. For instance, within some Indigenous communities, negative stereotypes linked to their native languages or cultural practices can deter younger generations from embracing their cultural roots. This reluctance often stems from the stigma attached to their identity by the dominant culture, leading to a gradual erosion of cultural practices and language.

Understanding the negotiation of identity during cultural transitions is crucial, as it explains why some ethnic groups may experience more tension and conflict with the host society than others. It also sheds light on the varying experiences within the same ethnic group, where some individuals may struggle with identity conflicts. In contrast, others find a harmonious balance between their cultural backgrounds.

The process of identity integration has profound implications for the broader society. A community cannot be truly cohesive and inclusive if immigrants do not feel a sense of belonging or cannot fully participate in the society's social, economic, and cultural life. Liu emphasizes that advancing our understanding of cross-cultural adaptation enriches intercultural communication theories and provides a foundation for developing programs that foster integration. These initiatives can catalyze positive social, psychological, and economic outcomes, ultimately enhancing society's ability to embrace diversity and maintain social cohesion.

Losing one's cultural identity in the context of cross-cultural engagement is a complex and often painful process that can occur when individuals, particularly immigrants or those from minority groups, immerse themselves in a dominant culture that may be vastly different from their own. This phenomenon is deeply intertwined with the challenges of integration, where the need to adapt to a new social and cultural environment can sometimes conflict with the desire to maintain a connection to one's original cultural heritage.

In cross-cultural engagement, individuals often navigate two or more cultural worlds, each with its values, norms, and expectations. This can lead to what is known as cultural dissonance, a state where the differences between the cultures create internal conflicts for the individual. The pressure to conform to the dominant culture—through language, behavior, or cultural practices—can be intense, leading some to lose touch with their original cultural identity gradually.

Berry's (1997) model of acculturation describes this process where individuals may undergo assimilation, which is a form of acculturation where they adopt the cultural traits of the dominant society while simultaneously losing aspects of their original culture. This loss can manifest in various ways, such as abandoning native languages, customs, and traditions in favor of those prevalent in the host society. Over time, this can lead to a weakening or even a complete erosion of cultural identity, leaving individuals feeling disconnected from their heritage and the new culture they are trying to embrace (Berry, 1997).

This process is further complicated by the broader societal context, where negative stereotypes and discrimination can exacerbate the loss of cultural identity. For example, research has shown that in some societies, minority groups may face pressure to conform to the dominant culture due to the stigmatization of their native languages or cultural practices. As Eades (2013) notes in the context of Indigenous communities in Australia, such negative perceptions can discourage younger generations from maintaining their cultural heritage, leading to a gradual decline in the use of native languages and practices. This is not just a loss of cultural identity but also a loss of the cultural richness these groups contribute to society (Eades, 2013).

The psychological impact of losing one's cultural identity can be significant. Individuals who feel they must relinquish their cultural roots to fit into a new society often experience a sense of identity confusion, loss, and alienation. This can lead to mental health issues such as depression and anxiety as the struggle to reconcile conflicting cultural identities takes a toll on their well-being (Ward, 2008). Moreover, losing cultural identity can create a disconnection from one's community and family, who may still uphold the original cultural values and traditions, leading to further isolation.

In contrast, maintaining a strong connection to one's cultural identity while engaging with a new culture can lead to what is known as a bicultural or multicultural identity. This form of identity allows individuals to draw strength and resilience from their cultural heritage while adapting to the new cultural environment. Research suggests that those who successfully navigate this balance tend to have better psychological well-being and are more effective in their social and professional engagements within the host society (Liu, 2017).

The loss of cultural identity in cross-cultural engagement is a significant challenge that requires careful consideration. Both individuals and societies must recognize the value of cultural diversity and create environments where people can integrate into new cultures without feeling compelled to abandon their original identities. By fostering bicultural or multicultural identities, societies can help individuals maintain their cultural roots while thriving in new cultural settings, ultimately leading to richer, more inclusive communities.

"The Salad Bowl"

In the 1960s, the metaphor of the salad bowl emerged to describe the American experience, where each ethnic group is like an ingredient in a salad, distinct yet harmoniously combined under the governance of the United States, symbolized by the dressing. Unlike the melting pot analogy, which suggests a blending of cultures into one, the salad bowl celebrates the preservation of cultural distinctiveness within a unified framework. This concept underscores the importance of fostering environments in organizations and communities that value diversity and inclusivity. By implementing inclusive policies, offering cultural awareness training, and encouraging intercultural exchanges, it is possible to create spaces where individuals from different backgrounds can thrive together.

The journey of bicultural individuals offers a unique lens into the complexity of identity. Being bicultural can be both empowering and disorienting. On the one hand, it allows individuals to draw from the richness of two cultural traditions; on the other, it can create tension when those cultures clash. There is no single definition of biculturalism because each individual's experience is deeply personal. For ethnic minorities, immigrants, interracial individuals, or those who have lived abroad, biculturalism is about more than adopting behaviors from two cultures—it involves merging cultural heritage with personal experiences to forge a distinct identity that reflects both origins and growth.

Biculturalism also intersects with the process of acculturation—the adaptation to a new culture. While acculturation was historically equated with assimilation, where individuals were expected to abandon their original culture to adopt the dominant one, modern frameworks, such as the bi-dimensional model, emphasize integration. This model highlights two simultaneous challenges bicultural individuals face: maintaining ties to their culture of origin while actively participating in the mainstream culture. Rather than marginalization, assimilation, or separation, integration fosters social and cognitive flexibility, enabling individuals to navigate diverse environments confidently. This balanced approach has been shown to protect against mental health challenges like anxiety and social issues such as intercultural misunderstandings.

A study by Yampolsky et al. (2013) offers valuable insights into how multicultural individuals construct and navigate their identities. The research reveals that those with an integrated cultural identity recount their life stories with greater coherence, which is strongly linked to well-being. In contrast, individuals who compartmentalize their cultural identities often struggle with fragmented self-concepts and experience lower levels of well-being. Interestingly, the study also found that individuals who identify primarily with one cultural identity can achieve narrative coherence similar to those with integrated identities. This finding suggests that comfort and familiarity with a single cultural alignment, often seen among second-generation immigrants, may foster a stable sense of self.

Choice plays a critical role in cultural identity formation. When individuals actively choose their cultural identity rather than having it imposed, they often experience greater well-being. This sense of agency contributes to psychological resilience and a stronger sense of control over their narratives. In inclusive societies like Canada, where multiculturalism and egalitarianism are celebrated, individuals may feel a greater sense of belonging and empowerment, further enhancing their well-being.

Adapting to new cultural environments involves more than a simple shift in behavior—it requires cultural intelligence (CQ), particularly CQ action. CQ action is modifying verbal and non-verbal behaviors to align with diverse cultural expectations. Unlike default responses, CQ action involves conscious adjustments that demonstrate sensitivity and awareness of cultural nuances. Research highlights the benefits of this adaptability, including improved negotiation outcomes, enhanced communication, and stronger cross-cultural relationships.

Behavioral adaptability is at the heart of CQ action—the ability to adjust speech, tone, and gestures to suit the cultural context. This skill encompasses knowing when to be formal or relaxed and how to make others feel comfortable. Beyond adaptation, it requires improvisation and reacting swiftly to unexpected cultural dynamics. By expanding their behavioral range, individuals can engage authentically with people from varied backgrounds while preserving their unique identity.

Both introverts and extroverts' approach CQ action differently, leveraging their strengths to navigate cultural interactions. Introverts often excel in deliberate, thoughtful adjustments, making them effective in environments requiring careful observation and planning. Extroverts, on the other hand, rely on social instincts to adapt quickly in fast-paced settings. Both styles highlight the multifaceted nature of cultural intelligence, which is not just about cultural fluency but also social fluency—the ability to interact gracefully in diverse environments.

For individuals from minority cultures, navigating between adaptation and preserving cultural identity can be challenging, particularly in environments where dominant norms overshadow minority traditions. This tension can lead to losing native languages, customs, and practices, with significant psychological consequences, such as alienation and identity confusion. However, successful integration does not necessitate abandoning one's roots. By blending cultural and emotional intelligence, individuals can honor their heritage while engaging meaningfully with new cultural contexts. This delicate balance enriches personal and social interactions, fostering a world that celebrates diversity and inclusivity

Reflection Questions
Chapter Nine

I. What are the most effective ways to modify one's behavior in real-time during cross-cultural interactions without overthinking or becoming too self-conscious?

_____

II. How can you develop the ability to apply their cultural knowledge and strategy into meaningful, adaptive actions in high-pressure or unfamiliar environments?

_____

III. How might you ensure your verbal and nonverbal communication aligns with the cultural norms of the people you interact with while maintaining authenticity?

_____

CHAPTER TEN

BIGGER THAN MYSELF

Growth Opportunities

I have been working my entire life, beginning at twelve or thirteen. Growing up, I attended public schools in districts far from the best—those prime schools were reserved for the middle and upper classes. However, even in these underfunded schools, occasional glimpses of hope existed. Every so often, the district would introduce model programs aimed at improving outcomes for children like me, the less fortunate.

One of these programs granted me a work permit and the chance to land a summer job. Each year, the opportunity arose, and I eagerly signed up, driven by the desire for independence. Having my own money meant having a say in my life, a chance to make decisions in a world where so much was out of my control.

My first job was as a porter in an Orthodox Jewish nursing home. Stepping into that world was like entering an entirely different universe, full of traditions and customs I had never known. I now wish I had embraced a profound cultural awakening more fully. Nevertheless, back then, I was focused on the work itself, and it was hard—especially for my thin, undeveloped body. I was young and inexperienced, still trying to figure out my place in the world.

The following summer, I found myself in a far less appealing situation. I was placed with the Army National Guard, a job that could only be described as miserable. There were two of us boys assigned to that site, and the only saving grace of the experience was the friendship we forged. Together, we endured long, grueling days in the mechanic's division, where they repaired and maintained the army's fleet vehicles. My job, as demeaning as it was, involved scraping thick grease from the wheelbases of the massive trucks. It was filthy, tedious work, and getting to the base each day required three bus transfers, followed by a bumpy ride in the back of a truck along dusty backroads.

The men at the base seemed to dislike me from the start. They were harsh and treated me with little regard, handing me the most unpleasant tasks as if I were some servant. One day, they sent me out to paint an old, neglected shed, which would have been simple enough if not for the hornet's nest I accidentally disturbed. I remember the swarm rushing at me, their stingers piercing my skin repeatedly. Only then, after seeing me in pain, did those men show any semblance of compassion, though I suspect they were more concerned about the liability than my well-being.

There were moments when I hoped for some respite from the drudgery—maybe even the chance to drive some of the vehicles, as my friend had been allowed. However, that opportunity never came. One day, he was driving a vehicle with a trailer attached, and he misjudged a turn, damaging the fender. Even though I was not behind the wheel, they blamed me for the incident. My friend tried to defend me, admitting his mistake, but they refused to believe him. They insisted I was at fault as if I were an easy scapegoat.

When I received my first paycheck, I did not spend it on myself. Instead, I bought gifts for my mom and little brother. I remember struggling with the weight of the packages as I made my way through the city, walking long distances between bus transfers. Thankfully, my program job counselor spotted me along the way and offered me a ride home. He smiled as I climbed into the car, playfully asking, "So, I see you are spending your first paycheck already. What did you buy?"

I explained that I had bought gifts for my family, and I could tell the gesture touched him. As we drove, he asked how things were going at my job, and I did not hold back. I told him everything—the grueling work, the harsh treatment, the unfair blame. His face grew serious as he listened, and I saw his concern. True to his word, he followed up, investigating my claims and finding them true.

He wasted no time searching for a new placement that would align better with my interests. I mentioned my love for art when he asked what I enjoyed doing. A week or so later, I found myself in a completely different world: working as a teacher's aide in a summer school class for second graders. My role was to help the children with arts and crafts, and I thrived in that environment. The teacher appreciated my efforts, and for the first time, I felt the joy of doing meaningful work that had purpose and impact beyond myself.

That summer was a turning point. It was the first time I truly understood that my efforts could touch the lives of others and that my work could be part of something larger than my struggles. In that classroom, surrounded by paint and construction paper, I realized that I had the power to make a difference. Moreover, that realization has stayed with me ever since.

What compels us to step outside of ourselves and work toward something greater? What motivates us to become "other-oriented," striving for a purpose beyond personal gain? This journey begins with empathy—learning to see through the eyes of others so that life may reveal a deeper meaning and purpose. What promise does life hold if we live solely for our advancement? Is existence itself enough without a higher calling? King Solomon once said, "I have seen all the things that are done under the sun; all of them are meaningless, a chasing after the wind" (Ecclesiastes 1:14, New International Version). Indeed, life can feel devoid of meaning when lived only for self-fulfillment. In those moments when we find ourselves depleted—when peace escapes us and an empty void seems to expand within—we begin chasing after anything to fill that space, whether it be a physical desire or a psychological craving.

As we journey through life, we often grapple with questions of purpose and meaning. Research by Warrell (2018) illuminates a powerful truth: those who connect to a purpose beyond the confines of their ego and ambitions—beyond the mere pursuit of power—experience a richer, more fulfilling existence. These individuals are happier, more content, and equipped with a profound resilience that sustains them through adversity. Our true calling lies not in titles or grand gestures but in the small, authentic ways we use our gifts to uplift others and improve the human experience.

Through the lens of cultural intelligence, we begin to see that our impact is magnified when we understand the diverse perspectives and needs of those around us. Cultural intelligence enables us to use our talents with sensitivity and awareness, acknowledging that everyone in each community has unique challenges and strengths. By cultivating this intelligence, we move beyond simply doing good—we elevate our contributions to a level that honors the complexity of human experiences.

As you look ahead to the unwritten chapters of your life, I encourage you to consider your options through the lens of personal gain and the wider scope of where you can make the most meaningful difference. How can your unique talents, hard-earned wisdom, and cultural understanding serve others in deeper, more impactful ways? The quest for meaning does not require direct pursuit. As Viktor Frankl wisely observed, true meaning flourishes when we devote ourselves to causes greater than our own lives—causes rooted in beauty, love, and justice.

The paradox of a meaningful life is that it often emerges when we focus on doing what is right. By committing ourselves to love fully, seeking diverse experiences, and engaging in tasks that matter not for self-validation but because they are good in themselves, we step into a life filled with purpose. The most profound sense of meaning blossoms in this space—where service to others and cultural intelligence intersect.

Our values are the compass that guides us, shaping how we find meaning and purpose in life. They are deeply woven into our actions and behaviors, the quiet but powerful force behind our choices. When life's challenges arise—when we encounter conflict or face obstacles that prevent us from living in alignment with what we hold dear—our sense of balance is often disrupted. Our actions can falter in these moments, and the behaviors that once flowed naturally may become strained or disconnected.

This tension exists not only within individuals but also across cultures. Each culture is built upon its unique set of values, which form the foundation of its worldview, norms, and way of interacting with the world. However, what one culture holds as sacred or essential may differ—sometimes drastically—from the values of another. This divergence can create friction, misunderstandings, or even outright conflict, as these cultural differences challenge the assumptions and beliefs each group holds dear.

Here is where the development of cultural intelligence (CQ) becomes transformative. Cultural intelligence allows us to move beyond seeing differences as threats or contradictions. Instead, it invites us to approach these differences with curiosity, understanding, and adaptability. By developing CQ, we learn to recognize the values that underlie our actions and those of others, fostering empathy for perspectives that may initially seem foreign or at odds with our own.

Imagine standing at the crossroads of two cultures, each with beliefs about what is meaningful and valuable. Without CQ, we might see only the conflict, focusing on what divides us. Nevertheless, with CQ, we can step into that space with open eyes, acknowledging that these differences are not barriers but opportunities for growth. Through this lens, cultural conflicts become less about right and wrong and more about understanding the deep values driving behavior.

When we embrace cultural intelligence, we can navigate the complexities of human interactions with greater ease and grace. We learn to balance our values with those of others, finding common ground where it might have seemed impossible. In this way, we deepen our understanding of the world and discover new layers of meaning in our lives—meaning enriched by the diversity of thought, belief, and experience we encounter.

Darryl Washington, D.Ed.

Sincerely Held Beliefs

Social change is a gradual yet dynamic process deeply rooted in transforming value systems that shape individual and collective identities. These value systems function as invisible threads, weaving through the lives of people and communities, binding their beliefs, principles, and choices into a cohesive whole. They represent what societies and individuals deem right or wrong, good or bad, and ultimately, what they hold most important. Shaped by cultural upbringing, social interactions, religious teachings, and personal experiences, value systems serve as compasses that guide decisions, actions, and judgments. However, they are far from static. Like living organisms, they evolve, adapting to new experiences, insights, and challenges that prompt a reassessment of priorities.

Understanding the interplay between stability and evolution within value systems is essential to comprehend the mechanics of social change. Transformative experiences—whether personal or societal—act as catalysts, encouraging embracing new ideas or reevaluating old beliefs. This process often manifests on a broader societal level, influencing societal norms, behaviors, and collective attitudes. However, this evolution is seldom linear. Societies frequently undergo a pendulum effect, oscillating between opposing extremes as they experiment with new ways of being before finding a more stable equilibrium. For instance, the 2024 United States presidential election highlighted intense cultural tension, where polarized ideals clashed in what many viewed as a cultural war. The ideological divide, rooted in contrasting value systems, stretched the nation's fabric to extremes, pitting leftist progressivism against right-wing conservatism.

This societal struggle can be viewed through Hofstede's dimensions, particularly the tension between individualism and collectivism. Individualism, which prioritizes personal freedom, autonomy, and self-expression, often clashes with collectivism, which values social harmony, interdependence, and group cohesion. These two ideologies shape societal structures and core values that define identity and purpose within a community. In the modern world, where diverse cultures interact, this clash has become a recurring theme, influencing debates about governance, education, and social justice. Over time, however, societies often move toward integrating these opposing values, seeking a balanced coexistence where individual autonomy complements collective well-being.

Hofstede's cultural dimensions provide a valuable framework for understanding the nuances of these shifts and their broader implications. Introduced in 1980, Hofstede's model captures the essence of societal values and their impact on behavior and norms. By exploring six key dimensions, the framework allows us to analyze cultural tendencies and their evolution over time.

1. **Power Distance Index (PDI):** Reflects a society's acceptance of hierarchical order. High PDI cultures respect authority and centralized power, while low PDI cultures emphasize equality and question authority. As societies evolve, a shift from high to low PDI often accompanies democratization and greater demand for egalitarianism (Hofstede, 1980).
2. **Individualism vs. Collectivism (IDV):** Individualistic cultures prioritize personal autonomy, while collectivist societies value group cohesion and loyalty. Economic development and globalization often nudge collectivist societies toward individualism, as greater

wealth enables individuals to focus on self-expression and personal goals (Hofstede, 1980; Inglehart & Baker, 2000)].

3. **Masculinity vs. Femininity (MAS):** Masculine cultures prize competitiveness and material success, whereas feminine cultures value the quality of life and nurturing relationships. Social change here often involves a move toward balance, with gender roles becoming less rigid.
4. **Uncertainty Avoidance Index (UAI):** Measures a society's tolerance for ambiguity. High UAI cultures prefer strict rules, while low UAI cultures are more open to change. Innovation and globalization can challenge high UAI norms, fostering flexibility and adaptability (Hofstede, 1980; Inglehart & Baker, 2000)].
5. **Long-Term vs. Short-Term Orientation (LTO):** Long-term-oriented societies focus on future rewards, while short-term-oriented societies prioritize tradition and immediate results. As societies modernize, they may lean toward long-term thinking, emphasizing sustainability and future planning (Hofstede, 1980; Inglehart & Baker, 2000)].
6. **Indulgence vs. Restraint (IVR):** Indulgent cultures embrace freedom and enjoyment, while restrained cultures regulate gratification through social norms. Economic prosperity often leads to increased indulgence, reflecting higher levels of individual satisfaction.

Hofstede (1980) argued that these cultural dimensions exhibit remarkable stability rooted in historical and ecological contexts. Social institutions such as family, religion, and education reinforce these values, crystallizing them over time. Nevertheless, external forces—modernization, globalization, and technological advancement—can challenge entrenched norms, leading to gradual but meaningful change. For instance, the rise of digital connectivity has exposed even the most isolated communities to diverse worldviews, encouraging cultural convergence and adaptation.

The modernization theory proposed by Inglehart and Baker complements Hofstede's insights, emphasizing how societies transitioning from industrial to post-industrial economies experience value shifts. Wealthier societies often prioritize self-expression, autonomy, and innovation, mirroring changes in Hofstede's dimensions like reduced Power Distance and lower Uncertainty Avoidance. However, these transitions are not without tension. Rapid change can feel destabilizing, leading to resistance or regression as communities struggle to reconcile the new with the familiar (Inglehart & Baker, 2000).

Cultural imperialism further complicates the landscape of social change. Western media, global brands, and consumerist ideals often impose dominant narratives on marginalized cultures, threatening the continuity of indigenous traditions. The pervasive influence of Hollywood films, American television, and brands like McDonald's and Coca-Cola reshapes local identities, eroding unique cultural expressions. This dynamic disrupts heritage and diminishes the sense of belonging derived from cultural roots. The homogenization of global culture risks replacing the richness of diversity with a monolithic narrative, leaving many voices unheard.

To counteract this, embracing the "Live and let live" philosophy becomes vital. These principals advocate respecting and celebrating diverse value systems rather than imposing one's own. It encourages communities to protect their heritage while remaining open to the insights offered by other cultures. By fostering mutual respect and understanding, we create a world where diversity is not seen as a threat but as a strength—a testament to the resilience and creativity of humanity.

The pendulum of social change reminds us that shifts in value systems are inevitable and necessary for growth. Understanding the factors that drive these changes—whether through Hofstede's dimensions or the pressures of globalization—equips us to navigate them with empathy and purpose. By balancing the push for progress with preserving cultural integrity, societies can evolve in ways that honor their past and potential. Through dialogue, mutual respect, and an unwavering commitment to justice, we can build a future enriched by the vibrant tapestry of human diversity.

Globalism or Culturally Distinct?

We are standing at the threshold of an age where the world seems to be shifting toward a monolithic order that prioritizes uniformity over preserving what makes us culturally distinct. In this emerging era, the formation of civilization often rests on the foundations of standardization—where people collectively agree that "this is how we live." However, this pursuit of a singular way of life comes at a cost: the rich diversity of human culture is slowly being eclipsed by a drive for homogenization.

Historically, civilizations have been shaped by clashes, conflicts, and wars, often sparked by cultural differences. From ancient tribal battles to modern geopolitical struggles, humanity has consistently found itself at odds with what is unfamiliar, what lies beyond its understanding. However, why do we, as humans, seem to oppose what is different inherently? What about the foreign, the unknown, that stirs fear, even hostility within us?

Perhaps it is because, at our core, we seek security and belonging. The familiar offers a sense of safety, a grounding in the world. Our customs, traditions, and ways of life give us an identity, a place in the grand tapestry of existence. When faced with something that challenges that identity—be it a different set of beliefs, a contrasting worldview, or an unfamiliar way of life—our instinct is to defend what we know. This instinct has been hardwired through centuries of survival in an unpredictable world where the unknown often posed a threat.

Nevertheless, as we move further into this age of global connectivity, the world is becoming smaller. We are increasingly confronted with differences that can no longer be ignored. Cultures that were once distant and separate are now intertwined, brought together by technology, travel, and the rapid exchange of ideas. The question that looms over us is this: Will we continue to resist what is different, clinging to the safety of the familiar, or will we embrace the beauty of diversity and allow it to enrich our collective human experience?

The answer to this question will shape the future of our global society. If we choose the path of resistance, we risk a world where cultural conflicts and divisions deepen, where the drive for uniformity snuffs out the vibrant uniqueness of human cultures. However, suppose we choose the path of openness and acceptance. In that case, we can create a world where diversity is celebrated, where different ways of life are not seen as threats but as valuable contributions to the whole.

To navigate this crossroads, we must examine our biases and fears first. What is it about difference that unsettles us? How can we move beyond the instinct to oppose the unfamiliar and instead learn from it? The answers to these questions are not simple but crucial to building a world where cultural distinctiveness is honored rather than erased.

Darryl Washington, D.Ed.

Hear Differently: Sociopolitical Effects on Individual Psyches

Sociopolitical events have a deep and lasting impact on the human psyche, often leading to cultural suppression and influencing mental health, emotional well-being, and social behavior. Elections, protests, or policy changes serve as powerful stressors, triggering immediate feelings of anxiety and uncertainty. However, disengaging from these events or remaining uninformed can be equally corrosive. The sense of helplessness that follows inaction can gradually erode one's mental well-being, creating a vicious cycle of stress and isolation.

One of the most visible consequences of sociopolitical events is the exacerbation of ideological divides. As tensions rise, people often gravitate toward ideologies that resonate with their beliefs about authority, social order, and power inequalities. This polarization creates social fragmentation, straining personal relationships and deepening community divides. Major events like the 9/11 attacks offer stark reminders of how these occurrences leave lasting psychological scars, disrupting individuals' sense of security and diminishing their trust in societal structures. The trauma of such events reverberates across time, affecting mental health in profound and lingering ways.

To navigate these challenges, it becomes essential to understand the psychological toll of sociopolitical upheaval and develop strategies to manage it. Finding a balance between staying engaged/informed and protecting mental health. Fostering open dialogues that bridge ideological gaps and supporting those affected by traumatic events can mitigate some of the adverse effects. However, we must embark upon this challenge by "hearing differently."

FINDING CULTURAL ACUITY

Cultural intelligence (CQ) equips you with the ability to navigate and cope with sociopolitical divides by fostering empathy, understanding, and adaptability. In times of deep polarization and conflict, CQ becomes a powerful tool for bridging gaps, promoting dialogue, and finding common ground amid differing ideologies.

One of the core components of CQ is the ability to suspend judgment and approach situations with an open mind. In the face of sociopolitical divides, this skill allows you to engage with others from a place of curiosity rather than confrontation. Instead of immediately reacting to opposing viewpoints, CQ encourages you to ask questions, understand the underlying motivations, and find the cultural context that shapes someone's beliefs. This shift in perspective transforms potentially divisive interactions into opportunities for meaningful conversation.

CQ also enhances your ability to manage emotions in tense situations. When confronted with sociopolitical stressors, your heightened self-awareness enables you to recognize how your emotions are influencing your reactions. This awareness helps you regulate your responses, preventing emotional escalation and allowing you to approach conflicts with a level-headed, solution-oriented mindset.

Furthermore, your cultural intelligence helps you navigate the complex landscape of identity and belonging that often lies at the heart of sociopolitical divides. By understanding how cultural backgrounds influence people's values and beliefs, you can better appreciate the diversity of perspectives within your community. This broader understanding fosters inclusivity and makes you more effective at finding common ground, even in polarized environments.

Moreover, your CQ allows you to build bridges across ideological divides by fostering empathy and mutual respect. Recognizing the human experience behind political beliefs helps break down barriers and enables you to connect with others on a deeper level. Rather than seeing people as representatives of opposing ideologies, you see them as individuals shaped by their own experiences, which makes it easier to find shared values and aspirations.

In practical terms, your CQ can also guide you in developing strategies to cope with sociopolitical stress. By leveraging your cultural understanding, you can create safe spaces for open dialogue, encouraging others to express their views without fear of judgment. These spaces can serve as platforms for healing, where people can engage in constructive conversations and rebuild trust.

Cultural intelligence cultivates resilience in the face of uncertainty. By embracing diversity and valuing different perspectives, you become more adaptable and less likely to be overwhelmed by the challenges posed by sociopolitical turmoil. Instead of feeling paralyzed by division, your CQ empowers you to act as a bridge between communities, fostering understanding and encouraging positive change amid conflict.

In essence, cultural intelligence equips you to navigate sociopolitical divides and empowers you to become a catalyst for unity, meaningful dialogue, and healing. By fostering empathy, adaptability, and a deep commitment to understanding, CQ enables you to contribute to a more inclusive and compassionate world, even in profound sociopolitical challenges.

As you cultivate cultural intelligence, you also develop cultural acuity—the keen ability to perceive and respond to the nuanced dynamics of different cultural contexts. This acuity sharpens your awareness of the complex layers that shape human behavior, allowing you to approach sociopolitical issues with greater insight and sensitivity.

FINDING CULTURAL ACUITY

Through this heightened understanding, you become more adept at finding common ground, facilitating conversations that bridge divides, and fostering environments where diverse perspectives can coexist and thrive.

Reflection Questions
Chapter Ten

I. What deeply held beliefs or assumptions might unintentionally reflect a bias toward others, and how can you approach addressing them in a way that is respectful and inoffensive?

_____

II. Are there any values or beliefs you feel may no longer serve you or align with your growth, and how might letting go of them impact your perspective or interactions with others?

_____

III. In what ways have you, your family, or your friends been affected by social-political events?

_____

ABOUT THE AUTHOR

Darryl Washington, DEd, is an educator and psychologist with over two decades of experience in human services. Drawing from his professional background and personal journey, Darryl's work centers on helping individuals negatively impacted by bias. His upcoming book is designed to provide practical tools and insights for those struggling to overcome the emotional and social effects of bias while also offering a compassionate perspective to those who may have unintentionally imposed bias on others.

With a deep commitment to fostering empathy and understanding, Darryl empowers readers to reflect on their experiences and behaviors, guiding them toward a more inclusive and supportive approach to life. He hopes to inspire meaningful change by bridging divides and promoting a more equitable, compassionate society.

NOTES

1. M. Adikwu, "The mental health costs of code-switching," Talkspace, January 29, 2020, https://www.talkspace.com/blog/code-switching-what-is/

2. A. Allen, M. L. Kern, C. S. Rozek, D. McInerney, and G. M. Slavich, "Belonging: A review of conceptual issues, an integrative framework, and directions for future research," *Australian Journal of Psychology* (2021), 73(1), 87–99, https://doi.org/10.1080/00049530.2021.1883409

3. M. Barreto and N. Ellemers, "Detecting and experiencing prejudice. Advances in Experimental Social Psychology," (2015), * 139–219, https://doi.org/10.1016/bs.aesp.2015.02.001

4. S. Bećirović, "The relationship between cooperative learning, cultural intelligence, EFL motivation and students' performance: A structural equation modeling approach," SAGE Open (2023), 13(4), https://doi.org/10.1177/21582440231208975

5. J. W. Berry, "Immigration, acculturation, and adaptation," *Applied Psychology* (1997), 46(1), 5–34.

6. Breadcrumb. (2023). The Behavioral Scientist. https://www.thebehavioralscientist.com/glossary/value-system

7. K. Bryc, E. Y. Durand, J. M. Macpherson, D. Reich, and J. L. Mountain, "The genetic ancestry of African Americans, Latinos, and European Americans across the United States." *The American Journal of Human Genetics* (2015), 96*(1), 37–53, https://doi.org/10.1016/j.ajhg.2014.11.010

8. V. Chávez, "Cultural humility and social inclusion." *Handbook of Social Inclusion* (2021), 1–16. https://doi.org/10.1007/978-3-030-48277-0_7-1

9. A. Clark, "Whatever next? Predictive brains, situated agents, and the future of cognitive science." *Behavioral and Brain Sciences* (2013), 36(3), 181–204.

10. L. R. Crutchfield, *How Change Happens: Why Some Social Movements Succeed While Others Don't* (Wiley, 2018).

11. B. De Martino, "Frames, biases, and rational decision-making in the human brain," *Science* (2006), 313 (5787), 684–687, https://doi.org/10.1126/science.1128356

12. T. L. Dixon, K. R. Weeks, and M. A. Smith, "Media constructions of culture, race, and ethnicity," *Oxford Research Encyclopedia of Communication* (2019). https://doi.org/10.1093/acrefore/9780190228613.013.502

13. Dr. Margie Warrell, "Pursue a Cause Greater Than Yourself: The Heart of True Leadership," *Forbes*, 2018, https://www.forbes.com/sites/margiewarrell/2018/12/08/why-doing-good-is-ultimate-success-strategy/

14. D. Eades, *Aboriginal Ways of Using English* (Aboriginal Studies Press, 2013).

15. D. S. Fleur, B. Bredeweg, and W. van den Bos, "Metacognition: ideas and insights from neuro- and educational sciences," *npj Science of Learning* (2021), 6 (1), 1–11, https://doi.org/10.1038/s41539-021-00089-5

16. D. V. Dixon, T. M. Azocar, and M. L. Casas, "The continuing impact of mediated stereotypes on racial attitudes: A longitudinal analysis of representations and their effects," *Journal of Communication*, 69(5), 800–818 (2019). https://doi.org/10.1093/joc/jqz019
17. E. K. Foster, "Research on gossip: Taxonomy, methods, and future directions," *Review of General Psychology* (2004), 8, 78–99.
18. A. Haesler, "Georg Simmel – Norbert Elias – Alfred Sohn-Rethel." *Recherches Germaniques* (2020), 15, 205–215, https://doi.org/10.4000/rg.4226
19. P. Hinton, "Implicit stereotypes and the predictive brain: Cognition and culture in 'biased' person perception," *Palgrave Communications* (2017), 3 (1), https://doi.org/10.1057/palcomms.2017.86
20. A. S. Hofmeyr, "Japanese university student responses to intercultural scenarios: Contact strategies and perceptions of otherness," *International Journal of Intercultural Relations* (2022), 90, 73–85, https://doi.org/10.1016/j.ijintrel.2022.07.008
21. "How to Hold Your Beliefs in a Healthy Way," *Psychology Today*, 2024, https://www.psychologytoday.com/us/blog/healthy-minds/202403/how-to-hold-your-beliefs-in-a-healthy-way
22. "Identity Crisis: Navigating biculturalism," *Psychology Today*, 2022, https://www.psychologytoday.com/us/blog/mind-matters-menninger/202201/identity-crisis-navigating-biculturalism
23. A. Jalata, "Revisiting the Black struggle: Lessons for the 21st century," *Journal of Black Studies* (2002), 33 (1), 86–116, https://www.jstor.org/stable/3180990

24. D. Kavanagh, G. Lightfoot, and S. Lilley, "Are we living in a time of particularly rapid social change? And how might we know?," *Technological Forecasting and Social Change* (2021), 169, 120856, https://doi.org/10.1016/j.techfore.2021.120856

25. S. Kettler, "Fred Rogers took a stand against racial inequality when he invited a Black character to join him in a pool," *Biography*, June 24, 2020, https://www.biography.com/news/mister-rogers-officer-clemmons-pool

26. A. C. Krendl, E. A. Kensinger, and N. Ambady, "How does the brain regulate negative bias to stigma?," *Social Cognitive and Affective Neuroscience* (2012), 7(6), 715–726, https://doi.org/10.1093/scan/nsr046

27. S. Liu, "Understanding the process of identity negotiation in cultural transition," Intercultural Communication Studies (2017).

28. J. L. Martin and H. Kwon, "Festinger, Schachter, and Back's social pressures in informal groups," In B. Pescosolido, B. L. Perry, E. B. Smith, and M. L. Small (Eds.), *Personal Networks* (Cambridge University Press, 2021), 3–17, https://doi.org/10.1017/9781108616490.003

29. C. L. McCluney, K. Robotham, S. Lee, R. Smith, and M. Durkee, "The costs of code-switching," *Harvard Business Review*, November 15, 2019, https://hbr.org/2019/11/the-costs-of-codeswitching

30. D. S. Meyer, *The Politics of Protest* (Oxford University Press, 2015).

31. G. Nardini, T. Rank-Christman, M. G. Bublitz, S. N. N. Cross, and L. A. Peracchio, "Together we rise: How social movements succeed," *Journal of Consumer Psychology* (2020), 31 (1), 112–145, https://doi.org/10.1002/jcpy.1201

32. M. Otten, A. K. Seth, and Y. Pinto, "A social Bayesian brain: How social knowledge can shape visual perception," *Brain and Cognition* (2017), 112, 69–77.

33. C. W. Perdue, J. F. Dovidio, M. B. Gurtman, R. B. Tyler, "Us and them: Social categorization and the process of intergroup bias," *Journal of Personality and Social Psychology* (1990), 59 (3), 475–486, https://doi.org/10.1037/0022-3514.59.3.475

34. T. Porter, A. Elnakouri, E. A. Meyers, T. Shibayama, E. Jayawickreme, and I. Grossmann, "Predictors and consequences of intellectual humility," *Nature Reviews Psychology* (2022), 1, 1–13, https://doi.org/10.1038/s44159-022-00081-9

35. N. I. Raddatz, P. A. Raddatz, K. Sorensen, and K. Ogunade, "The adverse effects of the 'anticipation of racial discrimination' on auditors who are Black, Indigenous, or people of color (BIPOC): An exploratory study with research propositions," *Accounting Horizons* (2024), 38(1), 139–147, https://doi.org/10.2308/HORIZONS-2022-098

36. T. Ravilochan, "The Blackfoot wisdom that inspired Maslow's hierarchy," *Resilience*, June 18, 2021, https://www.resilience.org/stories/2021-06-18/the-blackfoot-wisdom-that-inspired-maslows-hierarchy/

37. B. Renner, B. "Curiosity about people: The development of a social curiosity measure in adults," *Journal of Personality Assessment* (2006), 87(3), 305–316, https://doi.org/10.1207/s15327752jpa8703_11

38. N. Rojas, "Looking at how prejudice is learned, passed," *Harvard Gazette*, August 13, 2024, https://news.harvard.edu/gazette/story/2024/08/looking-at-how-prejudice-is-learned-passed/

39. K. Samuel, "The new psychology of belonging," *Psychology Today*, https://www.psychologytoday.com/intl/blog/the-power-of-belonging/202304/the-new-psychology-of-belonging

40. L. Shainis, How we can shift the power imbalance in adult education to deepen a sense of belonging, improve program outcomes, and create a more equitable society," *COABE Journal: The Resource for Adult Education* (2020), 9(2), 68–74.

41. R. J. Sternberg, S. K. Ang, and D. L. Heine, "Cultural intelligence in a globally connected world: Perspectives and challenges," *International Journal of Intercultural Relations*, 90, 45–57 (2022). https://doi.org/10.1016/j.ijintrel.2021.12.004

42. S. Sleek, "The bias beneath: Two decades of measuring implicit associations," *APS Observer* (2018), 31(2), https://www.psychologicalscience.org/observer/the-bias-beneath-two-decades-of-measuring-implicit-associations

43. D. Smiles, "Erasing Indigenous history, then and now," *Origins*, September 2021, https://origins.osu.edu/article/erasing-indigenous-history-then-and-now?language_content_entity=en

44. H. Song, A. Varma, and Y. Zhang Zhang, "Motivational cultural intelligence and expatriate talent adjustment: An exploratory study of the moderation effects of cultural distance," *The International Journal of Human Resource Management* (2021), 34(2), 1–25, https://doi.org/10.1080/09585192.2021.1966491

45. R. J. Sternberg, I. Siriner, J. Oh, and C. H. Wong, "Cultural intelligence: What is it and how can it effectively be measured?," *Journal of Intelligence* (2022), 10(3), 54, https://doi.org/10.3390/jintelligence10030054

46. The Decision Lab, "Attentional bias," The Decision Lab, https://thedecisionlab.com/biases/attentional-bias

47. "The Paradoxical Secret to Finding Meaning in Life," Psychology Today, 2018, https://www.psychologytoday.com/us/blog/supersurvivors/201805/the-paradoxical-secret-finding-meaning-in-life?msockid=3b3a1d4fb148660d06fd0fd4b0e067a5

48. R. Thompson, "A qualitative phenomenological study of emotional and cultural intelligence of international students in the United States of America," *Journal of International Students* (2018), 8(2), 1220–1255, https://doi.org/10.32674/jis.v8i2.144

49. M. A. Wahba and L. G. Bridwell, "Maslow reconsidered: A review of research on the need hierarchy theory," *Organizational Behavior and Human Performance*

(1976), 15(2), 212–240.

50. C. Ward, "Thinking outside the Berry boxes: New perspectives on identity, acculturation, and intercultural relations," *International Journal of Intercultural Relations* (2008), 32(2), 105–114.

51. D. Washington, "A mixed methods study exploring the prevalence of cultural suppression among international students studying at universities in the United States" (PhD diss., Oral Roberts University, 2017), ProQuest, https://www.proquest.com/pqdtlocal1005725/dissertations-theses/mixed-methods-study-exploring-prevalence-cultural/docview/1951781119/sem-2?accountid=12997

52. "What is a superiority complex?" Verywell Mind, Retrieved March 14, 2023, https://www.verywellmind.com/superiority-complex-causes-characteristics-and-coping-7095818

53. M. A. Yampolsky, C. E. Amiot, and R. de la Sablonnière, "Multicultural identity integration and well-being: A qualitative exploration of variations in narrative coherence and multicultural identification," *Frontiers in Psychology* (2013), 4, Article 126, https://doi.org/10.3389/fpsyg.2013.00126

54. W. Wood and A. H. Eagly, "Cultural influences on gender and behavior," *Psychological Bulletin*, 128(5), 699–727 (2002). https://doi.org/10.1037/0033-2909.128.5.699

55. F. Beugelsdijk, and A. Maseland, *Are Hofstede's culture dimensions stable over time?*, ResearchGate, (2019). Available at: https://www.researchgate.net/publication/333415773_Are_Hofstede's_culture_dimensions_stable_over_time.

56. H.-S. Lee, S. U. Chernikov, S. Nagy, and E. A. Degtereva, "The Impact of National Culture on Innovation: A Comparative Analysis between Developed and Developing Nations during the Pre- and Post-Crisis Period 2007–2021," *Societies* (2022), 11(11), 522, https://doi.org/10.3390/soc sci11110522.

57. S. Fischer and L. Poortinga, *Hofstede Dimensions and Their Validity in Cross-Cultural Psychology: A Meta-Analytical Perspective*, Frontiers in Psychology (2021), 12(662604), https://doi.org/10.3389/fpsyg.2021.662604.